DAY TRIPPER

TOKYO

Explore beyond the city with 50+ day trip destinations

Smith Street Books

Steve Wide
Michelle Mackintosh

LAKE ASHI, P 121

Tokyo never truly sleeps. It glows. It hums. It thrums with a pulse so bright and constant it feels almost alive – a neon heartbeat that flickers across glass towers and pumps life through the veins of endless streets. Crowds move like rivers through Shinjuku's steel canyons, while midnight ramen stalls hiss and steam in alleys that never darken. The Yamanote Line circles on, unblinking. Here, time stretches and folds; morning becomes night without warning, and the city is a shimmering loop of energy, appetite and invention.

But even in a city that has everything, there comes a moment when the senses crave silence – when the body, tuned to the metropolis's electric rhythm, longs for another kind of sound: the whisper of wind through bamboo; the lap of water against a quiet shore; the creak of a temple gate beneath the trees.

That's where this book begins.

Because one of Tokyo's greatest wonders is how easy it is to escape when you need to.

Step aboard a train and within an hour or two you can trade skyscrapers for cedar forests, LED billboards for temple lanterns and the scent of yakitori smoke for sea spray. The miracle of Japan's rail and bus networks means that the world beyond Tokyo isn't a faraway dream – it's a living, breathing extension of the city itself.

You can wake to Shibuya's or Shinjuku's mad rush and by lunchtime find yourself standing on a misty mountain trail, moss soft underfoot. You can leave behind the footsteps of shoppers in Ginza's glimmering boutiques and follow the ancient footsteps of pilgrims and samurai, or wander through fishing ports where the morning's tuna still gleams with ocean salt. You can end your day in an onsen town, soaking beneath stars reflected in hot spring waters. It's so close you can touch it, the full symphony of Japan: the thunder of waterfalls in Okutama; the quiet devotion of Shibamata's temples; the salty wind of Katsuura's coast; the warm hum of sake breweries and soy sauce factories still alive with centuries of craft.

•

Let us introduce ourselves: we are Steve Wide and Michelle Mackintosh and we are passionate Japanophiles, visiting Tokyo and beyond many times over the past 25 years. We spend three months of each year floating around our favourite country, uncovering beauty and history, eating our way through the seasons and enthusiastically seeking out small towns with a history of craft, generational stores and regional specialties. Mindfulness is always at the top of our travel agenda, so when visiting Tokyo we look for day trips to slow our pace and uncover lesser-known experiences. Michelle loves to participate in craft classes, visit vintage stores for local, handmade treasures and uncover local customs. Steve rifles through racks of vintage vinyl, digs out the best seasonal bites and hunts for the quirkiest regional mascots.

DayTripper: Tokyo was born from that feeling – the joy of escape without departure. It's a guide for those who want to adventure beyond Tokyo's borders and yet, most of the time, still be back in time for dinner.

We've curated a selection of our most-loved day trips – trips that you won't always find in other guidebooks. Whether you have a free day, the sudden urge for an unplanned adventure or simply the curiosity to follow the next train to wherever it takes you, this book invites you to step outside the city's edge and discover the world that exists beyond.

Because sometimes, the best way to fall in love with Tokyo all over again is ... to leave it. And when you return, the city feels like a familiar friend, welcoming you back with open arms.

WHY DAY TRIP?

On every trip we take to Tokyo (and there have been more than 60 so far), we make a detour. Heading out of the city, even just for one day, always makes our trip culturally richer. We travel for distinct reasons: the pottery fair in Mashiko to buy handmade ceramics and to visit special friends; the Bonsai Museum in Omiya on the cusp of spring or summer to view tiny camellia trees in bloom (and so Steve can visit one of his favourite ramen joints); Nasu-Shiobara in winter for a rustic onsen (and dairy products at the station) – the list goes on and is ever-evolving, making our Tokyo trips even more memorable.

We highly recommend venturing further out. Japan is diverse and varied, and can change quite dramatically within a journey of 1 or 2 hours, presenting you with unexpected and vibrant experiences beyond the city's frame.

Even close to the capital, small cities beckon, each one bursting with its own local culture. Many of Tokyo's day trip options are the blockbuster destinations most people know; we include a number of these but offer a more personal and nuanced approach to the experience. Others we've included are lesser known but by no means less enriching.

There are many reasons to go on a day trip; here are some of our favourites.

MINDFULNESS & NATURE

Stepping out of the concrete jungle into a forest, garden or far-flung temple will still your mind and soothe your travel-weary soul. Be intentional with your time and take the day slowly. Japanese nature is wondrous in every season – in winter, some of our favourite things include temple visits in snowy landscapes and steaming bowls of udon.

SEASONS

Japanese seasons are distinctive: a hot, humid summer; a crisp winter with bright blue skies; a spring filled with blossoms; and an autumn with maple and ginkgo trees painting the landscape in golds, oranges and reds. In the traditional Japanese calendar, there are also 72 shichijuni ko (micro-seasons), which are worth researching before your trip. If you travel between 24 and 28 February, then you will be there for the poetic 'mist starts to linger' micro-season; if your trip coincides with 4–8 April, it will be the beautiful time of 'swallows return'. For more on Japan's seasons, see page 26.

BIKE & HIKE

Outside of Tokyo are many amazing trekking paths. Make sure you pack an outfit that makes your bike or hike comfortable. Mountains, woods, beaches or vistas, a day trip from Tokyo has a stunning array of options. For info on how to hire a bike, see page 23.

ADVENTURE

The Japanese countryside accessible from Tokyo is bursting with choices for wild nature adventures, walks, culture and more. Climb a mountain, trek to see snow monkeys, visit an open-air gallery.

PASSION

Travelling for your passions may be the reason you are visiting Tokyo in the first place, with city escapes providing unique experiences. Go to the source of your sake obsession or noodle love, learn a little about Japanese regional cuisine, or explore history, unique and spectacular gardens, regional art or impressive architecture.

HOW TO USE THIS BOOK

So you've booked your Tokyo adventure, and the excitement has begun. Now you're wondering if there's a way to experience a little more of Japan's rich culture while you're there. Well, this book is for you!

We've structured the book by region – Outer Tokyo, North, South, East and West – and designed the pages so you can dip in and out to discover the day trips that most appeal to you. Once you've found your shortlist, narrow it down to your favourites based on what you're interested in and how much time you have.

From there, you can focus on the details of that particular adventure to best work out how to travel there and what not to miss once you arrive.

We offer suggestions on what to take, how to get around, the main focus of each area and the best seasons to visit. We've included trips for foodies, lovers of culture and art, and those who enjoy the great outdoors or want to discover spectacular coastal or mountain vistas. All you have to do is find something that appeals to you and then start planning.

NAVIGATING YOUR DAY TRIP

SYMBOLS

Throughout the book you will notice that each listing includes symbols that highlight different activities. We've developed the below key to help you decide on the best trips for your interests.

TRIP INFORMATION

Transport information is listed at the beginning of each day trip. The travel time for each trip is listed after the mode of transport. Depending on where you are staying in Tokyo there may be a quicker way to reach your destination.

- Shinkansen train
- Local or express train
- Change to a local or express train
- Bus
- Taxi
- Cable Car
- Ferry
- Walk

Times between connections have not been calculated. (Bus, Taxi)

GETTING THERE
Public transport information

STATION EXIT
Particularly useful for larger stations

WEBSITE
Where possible, we've included location websites, as this is a great way to research current events, plan lunch options and make sure the venue is open the day you visit (especially if it is a public holiday in Japan)

DISCOVER
Main points of interest (the things we think you'll love; not all the main tourist attractions)

SEASONAL HIGHLIGHTS
To help you plan the timing of your visit

ADVICE
Anything we think will make your trip smoother or more interesting

POPULAR DAY TRIP THEMES

KANAYA-ZAKA ON THE OLD TOKAIDO ROAD, P 126

ARCHITECTURE

Samurai Echoes in Matsudo, p 60
Little Edo in Kawagoe, p 34
The Kadokawa Musashino Museum, p 54
Nihondaira Yume Terrace, p 98
Holy Karuizawa, p 188
See all art listings!

ART

Kurkku Fields, p 152
MOA Museum of Art, p 116
Odawara Art Foundation Enoura Observatory, p 118
Art in Gora, p 124
Hara Museum ARC, p 196
evam eva yamanashi, p 176
Kubota Itchiku Art Museum, p 200

CRAFT

Pottery in Mashiko, p 74
Omiya Bonsai Art Museum & Village, p 40

GARDENS

Hitachi Seaside Park, p 84
Kairaku-en Garden, p 88
Showa Kinen Park, p 48

POP CULTURE

Moomin Worlds, p 50
Ghibli Pilgrimages, p 62
Retro Ome, p 58
Vintage Kamakura, p 132
Nostalgic Shibamata, p 46
The Kadokawa Musashino Museum, p 54

RELAX

Shibu Onsen, p 182
Coastal Kamogawa, p 162
Kamogawa Onsen, p 164
Breezy Katsuura, p 158
Shika-no-yu Onsen, p 86
Shuzenji Onsen, p 106
The Sea & Steam of Atami, p 114
Ikaho Onsen, p 198
Kusatsu Onsen, p 194

NATURE WALKS

The Old Tokaido Road, p 126
The Nakasendo: Magome to Tsumago, p 184
Spiritual Chofu, p 36
Mount Omuro, p 108
Karuizawa Nature Walk, p 192
The Steaming Valley of Jigokudani, p 180
Miho No Matsubara, p 102
Mishima, p 104
Volcanic Hakon, p 120
Lake Kawaguchi, p 202
Adventures in Chichibu, p 206

BIKE

Showa Kinen Park, p 48
Miho no Matsubara, p 102
Hitachi Seaside Park, p 84

SPIRITUAL

The Temple Town of Narita, p 148
Spiritual Chofu, p 36
Holy Karuizawa, p 188
Merciful Takasaki, p 174
Sunosaki Shrine, p 156
Zen Kamakura, p 128

HIKE

Mount Oyama, p 204
Chichibu Pilgrimage Day Walk, p 214
Gentle Okutama, p 42
Hiking Mount Takao, p 52
Nikko's Lake Chuzenji & Senjogahara Marshlands Day Walk, pp 78–83
Mount Nokogiri, 154

HISTORY

Samurai Echoes in Matsudo, p 60
Sacred Sites in Utsunomiya, p 70
Little Edo in Kawago, p 34
Nostalgic Shibamata, p 46
Historic Nikko, p 76
Izukyu-Shimoda, p 112
Daruma Dolls in Takasaki, p 172
Mount Nokogiri, p 154

FOOD & DRINK

Gyoza in Utsunomiya, p 168
Breezy Katsuura, p 158
Chichibu Sake, p 209
Wineries in Yamanashi & Kofu, p 178
Tea In Shizuoka, p 94
Noodles in Yokohama, p 136
Miura & Jogashima Island, p 138
Kikkoman Soy Sauce Factory & Museum, p 166
evam eva yamanashi, p 196

REGIONS & PLANNING

The majority of the day trips in this book are centred around the Kanto region and, to a lesser extent, the Chubu region. We also make some Weekend Tripper suggestions (see page 216), which dip into the Hokuriku and Kansai regions and go further into the Chubu region.

Large cities, prefectures and Shinkansen routes can be viewed on this map. To help you plan, it's important to find your bearings before you leave and make sure you know where the main train lines go and how close day trips are to one another. This will also help you plan overnight or weekend adventures if you are keen for more time out of the city.

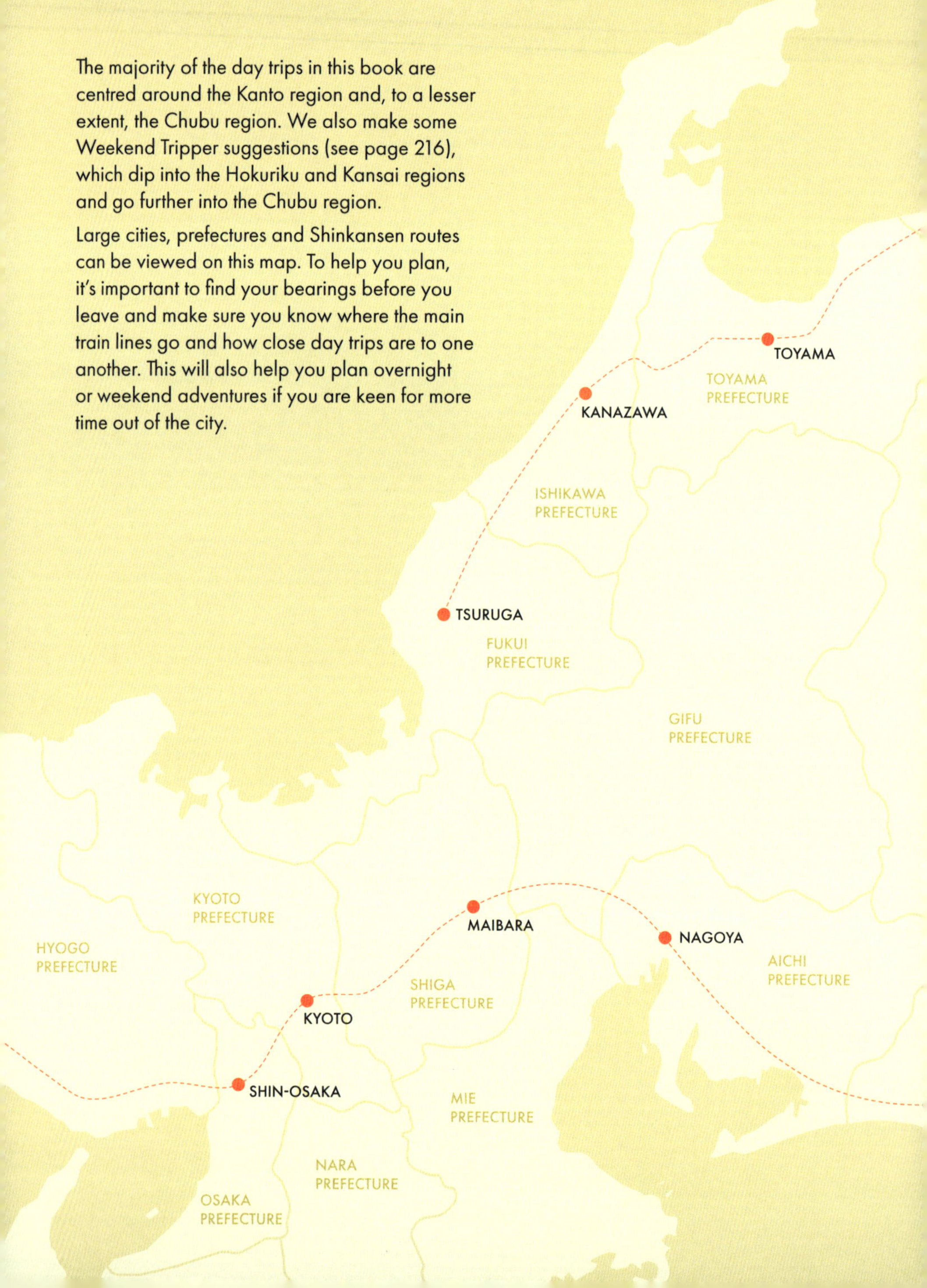

TO
NIIGATA
FUKUSHIMA
PREFECTURE
NIIGATA
PREFECTURE
NASU-SHIOBARA
ECHIGO-YUZAWA
TOCHIGI
PREFECTURE
NAGANO
GUNMA
PREFECTURE
UTSUNOMIYA
TAKASAKI
KARUIZAWA
IBARAKI
PREFECTURE
NAGANO
PREFECTURE
SAITAMA
PREFECTURE
OMIYA
UENO
TOKYO
METROPOLIS
YAMANASHI
PREFECTURE
TOKYO
KANAGAWA
PREFECTURE
CHIBA
PREFECTURE
SHIZUOKA
PREFECTURE
MISHIMA
ATAMI
SHIZUOKA
KAKEGAWA
SHINKANSEN
TOKYO
MAJOR SHINKANSEN
STATIONS
MOUNT FUJI

TRANSPORT

HANNO STATION

CALCULATING TIMES & CHOOSING TRANSPORT

Once you have decided on your day trip, check your transport options. Most of the adventures in this book begin at Tokyo or Shinjuku stations, with the occasional one departing from Ueno or Ikebukuro stations. However, Tokyo is a vast city and it can take 40 minutes to travel from one side to the other. So, depending on the location of your accommodation, your trip may be longer or shorter than the times we've listed. The best thing to do is to check your route online by using a website such as hyperdia.com or japantravel.navitime.com (simply input your start and end stations). This will give you a more accurate trip time based on your nearest station, and it will also show you the schedule for express trains, which will make your travel experience smoother.

Many of our day trips have multiple paths to the destination, so you'll usually have options. There may be several private train companies as well as Japan Rail (JR) offering transport. You may also have a bus option and, in some cases, a ferry option. For some places, it will be easier to use bikes or taxis to get there. In short, we'll give you the best options, but we also encourage you to do your own research to find the best times and transport for you.

PACING YOURSELF

We love to challenge our rail/bus pass to see what we can fit into a day while travelling, setting out early to really make the most of our destination. We choose a place with one thing we're excited about, and if time allows, we also look for a walk, local crafts, the town's lunch specialty or exhibitions in a gallery. We always talk to local volunteers or station staff and ask for their recommendations. The destinations we choose often include an onsen or a notable temple, adding culture and mindfulness to our day.

Tackling the day at your own pace is paramount. While we love to fit in as much as possible, you may opt for a slower pace. For each day trip, we list all the things to do, understanding that perhaps only one or two things may be realistic. Don't forget, you can always choose to stay overnight or for a couple of days. Many of our day trips feature experiences that are near each other so we've noted when it's worth staying in the area to do two, or even three, memorable things. Revisit the map at the start of each chapter to see which day trips are close to one another. Remember, though, that the train and bus networks will shape your day, because sometimes, even if places look close together, they may not have a connecting public transport route.

Another convenient way to combine day trips is to hire a car.

Here are a few sample itineraries for combining day trips:

* Kamakura Zen temples (page 128) with Kamakura vintage shopping (page 132) and Enoshima (page 134)
* Kawagoe (page 34) in the morning and Chichibu (page 206) in the afternoon
* MOA Museum of Art (page 116) or Odawara Art Foundation Enoura Observatory (page 118) in the morning and Atami (page 114) in the afternoon
* Nihondaira Yume Terrace and Kunozan Tosho-gu Shrine (page 99), with Miho no Matsubara (page 102)
* Oya History Museum and Wakayama Bamboo Farm (page71) with Utsunomiya gyoza (page 68)
* Mount Nokogiri (page 154) and Kurkku Fields (page 152).

Many of our trips require a bit of travel, yet for us the travel time is always worth it. For example, Kyoto and Osaka are both doable as a day trip from Tokyo – we have made the dash for a special exhibition, flea market or cultural event, or just because we felt like Kyoto pickles and tofu or Kanazawa seafood.

The trip can be expensive though, so it's perhaps only worth it if you have days left on your Japan Rail (JR) Pass or can buy a well-priced regional pass.

Other trips may take a bit of messing around with trains or buses, which can be frustrating at times. But it's well worth it – you will be visiting towns and places off the tourist track and you may find yourself the only one at a sacred temple, on a forest walk or in a gorgeous family-run noodle shop. Just remember to go easy on yourself and take the occasional taxi or hire a car when you need to.

OVERNIGHTERS & WEEKENDERS

Overnight and weekend trips are great because they give you the opportunity to really explore an area, perhaps combining two or three day trips into one weekend. They can also offer a richer experience, allowing you to enjoy a ryokan (Japanese inn) stay with an onsen (hot spring) and Japanese breakfast, or perhaps a dawn meditation class or a visit to an early-morning fish market.

Another reason may be that there is simply too much to see and do in the area, and you'd like to relax into your mini-break. Perhaps the train ticket or car hire becomes better value if you make good use of it with multiple experiences. For nature lovers, a weekend hike, multi-day walk or bike ride in the country might be a welcome change from Tokyo's pace. For those on a whirlwind trip away, it is still a wonderful idea to plan an overnighter if you can: spend a night among the mountains, detour for a 24-hour ramen challenge in Yokohama or cycle along the beach in Miho.

What about your luggage? Well, we like to be super-organised before we leave home: we book the same hotel for our entire Tokyo stay but leave one or two days out in the middle. We politely ask the hotel in advance if they are able to look after our bags for those one or two days so we can travel luggage free. If your accommodation is unable to care for your bags, a station locker or luggage-minding service (available at Tokyo Station and a few other 'hub' stations) is a great option.

If you're keen to plan some overnight stays, you'll see more ideas for overnighters in the relevant day trips.

Accommodation

Japan has many forms of accommodation, from ubiquitous business hotels (often around train stations) to places with sophistication, atmosphere and character.

A ryokan often has a communal bathhouse or onsen, with options for dinner and breakfast built in to the price. Housed in beautiful old buildings, often small in size, ryokan are known for their deep hospitality (omotenashi) – a rite of passage for the serious Japan adventurer. You will most likely share a bathroom and sleep on a futon on a tatami mat floor, just as travellers before you have done. Ryokan are near major ancient trade-route rest stops, deep in forests or mountains and even near major train station hubs. They will always reflect a region's specialties and history.

You may prefer to rent a tent and all your kit at one of Japan's glamping or camping sites (see japan.travel/en/guide/camping to discover a range of camping options). Facilities can include barbecues, food to purchase and sometimes sleeping lodges and an onsite restaurant. One example is the great glamping set-up at the base of Mount Omuro, called Forest Glamping Kanade no Mori Resorts. For many locations, the most convenient way to reach them will be to hire a car. Not all facilities have tents so it's best to check in advance.

Minshuku are stays in private homes and can be less expensive and more personal than staying in a ryokan. You'll be welcomed into a cosy environment with home cooking and a local's perspective. Why not try a home stay or farm stay for a deeper look into Japanese daily life (see japan.travel/en/guide/homestay-farmstay for options).

You'll find historic post towns between Tokyo and Kyoto, and the trails and roads are mostly preserved, making for amazing hikes. Walking the Nakasendo (see page 184) is a wonderful example of this. If you want to turn the experience into an overnighter, there are many old-school accommodation and ryokan providing both breakfast and dinner and possibly an onsen bath along the way.

GETTING THERE

We have chosen what we consider to be the best route for your day trip in terms of both time and cost. If there is another serious contender for the best travel mode, we mention it in the day trip's Advice section.

Planning ahead is wise as some routes will have optimal travel times or connections. Your destination may also offer options such as a Shinkansen, an express train or a bus.

Car

Hiring a car in Japan is a great way to see the countryside and travel to those places with a less predictable public transport schedule. For a relaxing day trip, take public transport out of Tokyo (driving in the capital can be stressful) and pick up your car at a major station outside of the city, closer to your destination. For example, one leisurely day trip with a hire car is to take the train to Nikko, pick up your car and drive to Lake Chuzenji. Another example is to take the train to Utsunomiya, pick up your car and drive to Mashiko, where public transport is infrequent and the town is harder to explore on foot.

Bookings can be made through online travel websites and also directly through car hire companies. Search the station you would like to hire a car from and choose an option.

Tips for driving in Japan

* Book your car in advance.
* You will need an international driver's licence.
* Japan has a strict almost-zero (0.03 per cent) blood alcohol limit for drivers.
* Please be aware of local road rules.
* Your GPS may not be in English.
* There may be tolls.
* Hire an electric vehicle for a lower travel carbon footprint.

Michi-no-Eki

Michi-no-Eki (roadside stations) are a seriously good reason to hire a car for a day. Think of them as a pitstop with benefits, a country konbini, or convenience store, with regional extras, a restful and mindful stop you will definitely want to make. Michi-no-Eki are set up to make sure drivers have opportunities to stretch their legs, and have become destinations in their own right, with excellent restaurants, multiple food choices, local produce and even local crafts. Government owned, they promote the region's bounty and are wonderful places to glean community knowledge. They range from rustic and basic to architectural marvels. Many have incredible food and some even have an onsen, such as Michi-no-Eki Okukuji Daigo in Ibaraki Prefecture.

Train

There are quite a few train passes that offer excellent value, making day trips achievable and economical. Their value might even make you rethink how many trips out of the city you'd like to take.

Trains in Japan are operated either by Japan Rail or one of a host of private railway lines. If you're thinking of buying a ticket, research the areas you plan to visit to see whether any of the following value passes fit your schedule. For example, if you buy a JR Pass you cannot use it on private railways.

We recommend buying tickets online in advance.

JAPAN RAIL DAY TRIP–FRIENDLY PASSES

https://japanrailpass.net; www.jreast.co.jp

There are a range of JR passes perfect for day trips. The regions of Japan are operated by different companies so it can seem a little confusing, but the above websites will give you options for most places.

NONBIRI Holiday Suica Pass

This is a good-value one-day pass for Kamakura, Tachikawa (Showa Memorial Park), Kawagoe, Omiya, Yokohama, Odawara (for Hakone), Chiba and more. You also have the option to buy a 'super limited express' add-on. Do your research though, as the cost of your pass may be more than a return ticket.

JR Tokyo Wide Pass

This three-day pass is great if you are planning longer trips, as it is valid on the Shinkansen to Karuizawa, Takasaki (for Ikaho Onsen), and Nasu-Shiobara. It is not valid on the Tokaido Shinkansen route (Tokyo to Kyoto route), which includes places such as Atami, Shizuoka and Mishima. It does include the Limited Express Odoriko Line to Atami, Izu and Izukyu-Shimoda, which is one of our favourite trains. But do check the schedule for this train as it has a limited number of journeys per day.

Other JR Passes

Japan Rail offers a slew of passes that, depending on your trip, can save you a lot of yen and take you to far-flung places. With Tokyo as a base, the above passes should suffice. If you are thinking of wandering further, the JR Hokuriku Arch Pass is a great buy, particularly if you want to do a Kyoto and Kanazawa weekender. The JR East Nagano Niigata Area Pass or the JR East Tohoku Pass offer great value for a colder climate mini-break. With these more expensive passes, remember to count the value not only in your weekend away but also in day tripping on JR lines closer to Tokyo.

PRIVATE RAILWAY PASSES

Seibu Railway Passes

www.seiburailway.jp

A private railway with a day trip hub at Ikebukuro Station, Seibu Railway has some of the best value passes for a plethora of diverse day trip options. A one-day pass is not to be missed! The one- and two-day options, Kawagoe Pass, Moomin Valley Park (train and park ticket), Chichibu Manyu Ticket and Chichibu Free Ticket are all excellent passes.

Odakyu Hakone Free Pass and Odakyu Enoshima Kamakura Pass

https://odakyu-global.com

This private rail line services two of Tokyo's best day trip areas. Buy digital tickets online.

* Hakone: a one-to-two-day pass includes discounts and all transport needed from Shinjuku to Hakone (including Lake Ashi Cruise and Hakone Ropeway at Owakudani). An extra fee is required for the Romancecar, which is quicker (a limited express) and slightly more comfortable (but please note that romance is not provided, so bring your own!).
* Enoshima Kamakura: this pass includes discounts and train rides from Shinjuku including the Enoden Electric Railway (page 135). An extra fee is required for the Romancecar.

Keio Railways Pass

www.keio.co.jp

This one-day pass from Shinjuku or Shibuya will take you to Chofu and Mount Takao.

Greater Tokyo Pass

https://greater-tokyo-pass.jp

This five-day pass offers fantastic value both for the price point and for the wonderful array of destinations you can visit: Yokohama,

Enoshima, Nikko, Narita, Chichibu, Shibamata, Chiba, Kawagoe, Mount Takao and more! Note though that this is a private railway pass valid on the train lines and buses specified. It is not valid on Japan Rail transport.

Day trip train hubs

Your day trip options will likely be influenced by the train hub you're nearest to and how much time you want to spend travelling. It may take only an hour on the Shinkansen to reach a destination far from the city. Or your journey may involve a series of local trains with multiple changes, making it essential to plan your connections properly. It also helps to mentally commit to the total journey time. For example, Tokyo to Kyoto on the Nozomi Shinkansen (the fastest) takes less time than taking local trains to the furthest parts of Chiba, despite Chiba being much closer to Tokyo.

Here are a few sample day trip destinations from key train hubs:

Shinjuku Station

* Odakyu Line Romancecar for Hakone
* Shonan Shinjuku Line for Utsunomiya
* JR Chuo/Ome lines for Ome
* JR Chuo Line for Showa Memorial Park.

Tokyo Station

* Tokaido Shinkansen for Atami, Shizuoka and surrounds, Kyoto and Osaka
* Hokuriku Shinkansen for Takasaki, Karuizawa and Kanazawa
* Joetsu Shinkansen for Niigata
* Odoriko lines for Atami and Izu Peninsula.

Ikebukuro Station

* Seibu lines for Kawagoe, Chichibu and Moomin Valley Park.

JR and Tobu Ueno stations

* Tobu train to Nikko
* Keisei Line for Narita and Shibamata
* JR express trains to Yokohama.

Local area transport passes

Many day trip destinations have combined bus, train and ferry passes. A great example of this is the three-day Mount Fuji Shizuoka Area Tourist Pass Mini (touristpass.jp/en/fuji_shizuoka). Offering brilliant value, it includes trains, buses and cruises. The itineraries for Kakegawa (page 95), Shizuoka (pages 94 and 98), Atami (page 114) and Shuzenji (page 106) fit this excellent pass and may inspire you to combine itineraries and turn this gorgeous part of Japan into a Tokyo mini-break.

Wherever you're going, it's worth checking with the tourist information office at your arrival station to see if a pass is available that suits your itinerary.

Bus

Bus rides are a comfortable and convenient way to reach your day trip destination, often offering lovely scenery and cosy seating. Tickets can be booked in advance, helping you plan your day and schedule. Some destinations may seem like quite the journey; however, once you've settled in and the big city disappears behind you, you'll be at your destination before you know it.

Some wonderful day trips require a tight schedule of hopping on and off trains and buses, but the most popular bus day trips are a smooth one-stop ride. A great example is visiting Kusatsu Onsen. The trip from Shinjuku Expressway Bus Terminal to Kusatsu Onsen usually requires two train rides then a bus, but the direct bus is cheaper and easier. However, for these longer day trips there may be only one or two bus departures a day (usually in the early morning) due to the length of the journey.

Bus bookings

Many companies offer highway bus journeys, so it's good to compare ticket prices and times. Conveniently, bus tickets can be booked online through japan-bus-tickets.com and willer-travel.com. Look out for the price difference between one way and return tickets, discounted tickets and days of the week when ticket prices are more affordable. Tickets can also be purchased at bus hubs (see below) and some JR train counters (if you are booking a JR bus).

A few things to note

* Bus hubs are near major train stations, making them convenient to find. Onboard amenities include a toilet, charging ports and air-conditioning.
* If you have a JR Pass, you can use most JR local buses; however, the pass is not valid on the JR highway bus.
* Train stations such as Tokyo and Shinjuku are home to large bus hubs. These stations are vast, so arrive early for your bus and make sure you have enough time to find the departure point. It can help to do a recce the day before.
* Popular destinations have more than one bus company vying for your business, so do check online for competitive prices. Also look for express services so you can arrive at your destination as quickly as possible.
* Up until recently the Pottery bus line for Mashiko ran twice a day, making it perfect for a day trip. Currently the bus is only running in the afternoon, so it's not right for a day trip but it's a great option for an overnighter, because it takes you from Tokyo Station to Mashiko – something that normally requires a few kinds of public transport and a bit of tenacity.
* You can eat on highway buses but it's polite to consider the food you are eating and whether it will impact others.
* For long journeys your bus will stop for a 15-minute bathroom and hydration break.

To give you a sense of how much time to allow, here are some sample bus travel times from Tokyo:

* Tokyo to Fuji-Q/Kawaguchiko (1 hr 50 min+)
* Akihabara to Fuji-Q/Kawaguchiko (2.5 hr+)
* Ikebukuro to Gotemba Outlets (Shizuoka) (1 hr 35 min+)
* Shibuya to Karuizawa (3 hr+)
* Shinjuku to Kusatsu Onsen (3.5 hr+).

Local town buses

Many day trip destinations have extensive bus networks, often with a day pass. A bus ride can be the very best way to see a town's beauty and meet the locals, and in these instances day passes offer great value and freedom. For example, Shizutetsu buses in Shizuoka offer a day pass; in Karuizawa you'll find both one- and two-day bus passes; and the Tokai bus company on the Izu Peninsula offers a variety of passes, taking you to places and spaces that trains cannot.

Day trip bus hubs

Here are the key bus hubs, if you're day tripping by bus:

Bus Terminal Tokyo Yaesu
https://bt-tokyoyaesu.com

This bus terminal is located underground at Tokyo Station's Yaesu exit. To reach it, once you're outside the Tokyo Station Yaesu south-side exit, follow the well-signed stairs down towards the bus terminal. The terminal has lockers, a convenience store and drink machines.

Bus Terminal Shinjuku (BUSTA)
https://shinjuku-busterminal.co.jp

This is the largest and most popular terminal.

Shibuya Mark City Bus Terminal (5F)
tokyubus.co.jp/tourist/shibuyabusterminal

Located on the fifth floor of the Shibuya Mark City complex, this bus terminal can be a bit tricky to find, so make sure you arrive early.

Ikebukuro Sunshine Bus Terminal
https://sunshinecity.jp/

You'll find this bus terminal on the first floor of the Bunka Kaikan Building.

Bus Terminal Akihabara
https://akiba.or.jp

This terminal is located out the front of Yodobashi Camera.

Airport limousine bus
www.limousinebus.co.jp
https://tyo-nrt.com/en

Tokyo has many limousine buses departing from locations all over the city that will connect you to both Narita and Haneda airports. For Tokyo Station to Narita Airport, the Tokyo Shuttle and Access Narita buses offer the greatest value. If you want an inexpensive way to visit Narita Town for the day (see page 148), take the shuttle bus then a local Keisei train to Narita.

Bike

Many country stations offer bike hire and, for us, taking a train or bus followed by a bike ride is one of our favourite ways to spend a day. Download apps such as LUUP (e-scooters and e-bikes), Hello Cycling or Docomo Bike Share to see hire spots and book a bike before you leave. Bikes often come in three sizes – small, medium and large – and electric bikes may be an option. Helmets are not mandatory in Japan but are strongly recommended by the government. We recommend always wearing a helmet for safety. However, helmets can be popular and may not be available on your day of hire. If you're a keen cyclist planning day trips with multiple bike rides, pack your own helmet along with your other cycling accessories for the best possible experience.

Taxi

Some of our day trip destinations are a little far from train stations. In these cases, you can catch a bus (though note that regional bus timetables may only have a service every 1–2 hours), hire a bike if available or take a quick taxi from outside the station. We always consider the shape of our day and the possibility that we may need to 'be kind to ourselves' and budget for a cab. Once when we were in Shizuoka, we took an affordable cab from the base of Kunozan Tosho-gu Shrine (page 99) to Miho Beach; the cab driver helped us explore different parts of Miho Beach and acted as a personal tour guide, so it was more than worth it.

Go Taxi App

Install this handy app before you leave for Tokyo, as it can be a real lifesaver if you are tired and on a country road with a long walk to or from your destination. In remote areas, a driver may not be nearby. However, if you happen upon a lone business or shop, they will often call a cab for you.

FESTIVALS

If you've never experienced a festival in Japan, we absolutely recommend you make it part of your day trip itinerary. Dancing, costumes, floats, parades and festive foods are just part of the excitement. Here, we list some of our favourite festivals. Please check dates online, as festivals are often on weekends and dates change slightly from year to year.

REGIONAL FESTIVALS THROUGHOUT THE YEAR

Japanese cities and towns pride themselves on having their own unique regional traditions, and for visitors, festivals can be a wonderful opportunity to understand differences between the areas surrounding Tokyo more deeply.

Regional festivals we love:

* Maebashi Hatsuichi Daruma Festival, January
* Katsuura Big Doll Festival, February–March
* Kamakura Festival, second Sunday in April
* Narita Gion Festival, early July
* Mishima Firefly Festival, mid-July
* Kawagoe Festival, select dates in October
* Chichibu Yomatsuri, early December

HATSUMODE (NEW YEAR'S EVE & NEW YEAR)

This is the first shrine visit of the year. Starting at midnight on New Year's Eve and lasting a few days into the new year, the ritual of Hatsumode shows gratitude for the past year and welcomes the year ahead. It's always very busy but extremely rewarding and festive.

Select shrines and temples to visit:

* Iseyama Kotai Jingu Shrine, Yokohama
* Naritasan Shinsho-ji Temple, Narita
* Shibamata Taishakuten Temple, Shibamata
* Tsurugaoka Hachimangu Shrine, Kamakura

NEW YEAR (JANUARY)

New Year in Japan is a time for family and preparing for the year ahead (including a deep clean of one's house). Look out for New Year's decorations strewn over doorways, kagami mochi (two stacked white mochi with bitter orange on top) and shimekazari (traditional rope decorations typically displayed over a door). Each region has its own unique take, so keep your eyes peeled. Special food is prepared for New Year in Japan, starting with soba noodles on New Year's Eve (long noodles for a long life), ozoni (vegetables and mochi in broth) and the elaborate osechi ryori (traditional New Year's dishes served in tiered boxes). Departo food halls are a great place to see osechi ryori, and also to marvel at how much they cost!

SETSUBUN (FEBRUARY)

This mamemaki (bean-throwing) festival involves throwing roasted fukumame (soybeans) at people dressed up as demons on temple and shrine grounds to ward off the previous year's evil spirits. It takes place around 3–4 February, on the last day of winter, and you'll find trinkets celebrating the festival, such as good luck charms, daruma dolls and blue or red devil masks, adorning pop-up street stalls. Banishing demons can be thirsty work, which means you can expect a lot of sake around these celebrations. Purchase a sake cup full of beans and a devil mask and you're good to go.

Select places to join in the festivities:

* Lake Ashi has fireworks by night, with celebrations the next day at Hakone Shine (page 121), including a demon on water skis, free sake and festive snacks.
* Mount Takao (page 52) is home to one of the best Setsubun festivals, at Yakuo-in Temple, in a beautiful woodsy mountain setting. Expect a fire ritual and possibly your favourite sumo wrestler on stage throwing beans as part of the celebrations. As Mount Takao is said to have no demons, this festival is all about bringing the good fortune inside without banishing the demons outside.
* At Jindai-ji Temple in Chofu (page 37), local onsen water is used to purify the beans. Festivities include a procession and the temple's famous Goma fire prayers.

I

'Oni wa soto! Fuku wa uchi!'
('Demons out! Fortune in!')

*

SETSUBUN CHANT

KOINOBORI (MAY)

Japan celebrates Kodomo no Hi (Children's Day), each year on 5 May, by flying bright, colourful carp streamers called koinobori. This festive visual feast decorates streets, parks and other outdoor spaces. Because Children's Day is part of Golden Week (when four national holidays fall within the same week), this is a very busy time of year to visit Japan, as the whole country is on holiday. Beat the Tokyo foot traffic and head out for a day trip to see more local celebrations.

Select places to join in the festivities:

* Himenosawa Park in Atami
* Kozunomori Park in Narita
* Showa Memorial Park
* Taisho Roman Yume dori in Kawagoe

I

Higher than the rooftops
are the koi-no-bori.
The large carp is the father.
The smaller carp are the children.
They seem to be having fun swimming.

*

CHILDREN'S CHANT

OBON (MID-AUGUST)

A sacred time of year in Japan, Obon is a three-day Buddhist festival that commemorates family and friends who have left this mortal coil. While it is a time of contemplation, towns and streets are often filled with an air of celebration. The Bon Odori (Bon dance), with beautiful costumes and spectacular moves, can be seen through streets and towns. Often accompanied by lanterns, the celebrations are both joyous and haunting. An important part of Obon is the Toro Nagashi (lantern festival), one of the most moving cultural events you will ever see. Dozens, if not hundreds, of tiny lit lanterns are set upon lakes, rivers and oceans to symbolise sending loved ones back to the afterworld.

Select places to experience Obon:

* Kamakura Beach Bon Odori Festival, Kamakura
* Minatomirai Dai Bon Odori, Yokohama
* Souen Shishi-Mai lion dance, Utsunomiya
* Toro Nagashi, Mishima

SEASONS

Japan has 72 shichijuni ko (micro-seasons), each lasting five days which fit neatly into the four regular seasons. All adorned with poetic names, these micro-seasons connect groups of days with budding flowers, the first sensing of snow, leaves changing colours, seasonal foods and festivals. Names can be evocative and charming, such as 'first rainbows', 'frogs start singing' and 'thick fog descends'.

From your base in Tokyo, day trip destinations can give you different seasonal adventures. For example, travelling north means you will greet winter earlier and autumn will be in October and early November rather than late November. The weather can actually change dramatically from place to place. Check the weather for your day trip destination in advance – you could have rain when Tokyo is sunny, or a sunny spring snap when Tokyo is still in winter mode!

KENROKU-EN GARDEN, P 237

OMIYA BONSAI ART MUSEUM & VILLAGE, P 40

SPRING (MARCH–MAY)

Spring brings some of our favourite foods: sakura mochi, soup and curry with mushrooms of all varieties, and young bamboo shoots. Fruit and vegetables are of an exceptional quality. This is the time to try local produce, especially outside of Tokyo where you may be buying from local growers and more grass-roots businesses. For example, Tochigi (see Mashiko on page 74 and Utsunomiya on page 68) is known for strawberries, and a strawberry soft-serve and strawberry juice in Shizuoka are a must (page 99).

For flowers and cherry blossoms, visit:

* Kairaku-en Garden (page 88) for cherry blossoms from late March to early April
* Showa Memorial Park (page 48) from late March to early April
* Takasaki (page 172) Spring Festival in the first week in April
* Hitachi Seaside Park (page 84) for blue nemophila (baby blue eyes) in mid-April.

SUMMER (JUNE–AUGUST)

Summer in Japan is very hot and humid and if you visit in early June to mid- to late July, you will also experience the rainy season. Both are extreme, so if we're travelling at this time, we plan indoor activities, forest bathing or escaping the summer heat by heading to the coast or going as far north as we can.

Japanese food is very seasonal. Summer dishes are simple and light and showcase fresh produce. Cold soba with dipping sauce is perfect for hot weather. We love salads with delicious dressings, and kakigori (shaved ice), parfaits and matcha soft-serve help keep you cool. Ice creams and drinks for hydration found at konbini (convenience stores) will at some point save your life. Of course, a cold Japanese craft beer or yuzu sour on a warm day is one of life's great simple joys.

To escape the summer heat, visit:

* Lake Chuzenji (page 78): Tokyo's summer heat was too much for European diplomats so they built their embassy summer villas on the cool shores of Lake Chuzenji. The Italian and British embassy villas on the lake are a must-visit for architecture buffs.
* Meigetsu-in (Hydrangea Temple) in Kamakura and the Hakone Tozan Line train (also called the Hydrangea Train) for cool respite (page 121)
* Hitachi Seaside Park (page 84) for green kochia and summery sunflowers
* Enoshima (page 134), Miho no Matsubara (page 102), Atami (page 114), Izukyu-Shimoda (page 112) and Katsuura (page 158) for wonderful seaside day trips.

AUTUMN (SEPTEMBER–NOVEMBER)

Autumn is our favourite time to visit Japan. Layered clothing and woolly walks in the woods make the season feel festive and cosy. Many temples, parks and gardens have autumn illuminations, and falling leaves rival cherry blossoms for displays of nature's vibrant colour palette. Our favourite things to eat are chestnuts, persimmons, sweet potatoes and shinmai (new rice).

For autumn leaves and nature, ideal spots include:

* Showa Memorial Park (page 48) for its Cosmos Festival from early September to late October, and its gorgeous ginkgo trees in mid-to late November
* Hitachi Seaside Park (page 84) for blue kochia in mid-October
* Nikko around Lake Chuzenji (page 78) from mid-October to early November
* Shizuoka's Inatori Hosono Kogen and its Pampas Grass Festival, from early to late November
* Shuzenji Niji no Sato Autumn Light Up, from mid-November to mid-December
* Ikaho Onsen (page 198) from late November to mid-December.

WINTER (DECEMBER–FEBRUARY)

Snowy day trips, winter flower in parks and chilly forest walks are all wonderful city sojourns. The weather around Tokyo is clear and crisp. We love to eat big bowls of steaming soba, udon, ramen, oden and Japanese curry. For desserts, zenzai (sweet red bean soup, often served with mochi) is a favourite. Winter is considered to be the season for sake, traditionally brewed during the colder months following the autumn rice harvest.

SNOW

Some areas around Tokyo may see snow in winter. From late November to early December, snow typically starts in Niigata, Karuizawa and Nasu Shiobara, with skiing accessible in Karuizawa, Niigata and Fukushima.

SNOWY ONSEN

If you're keen on bathing in hot springs in the snow, try:

* Ikaho Onsen (page 198)
* Jigokudani Snow Monkey Park, Yudanaka (page 181)
* Kusatsu Onsen (page 194)
* Shika-no-Yu Onsen, Nasu-Shiobara (page 86)
* Shuzenji Onsen (page 106).

EARLY CHERRY BLOSSOMS

Atami (page 114) has a variety of cherry trees (Atami zakura) that blossom early. From January to early February, Itokawa Promenade and the Atami Plum Garden both have spectacular displays.

PLUM BLOSSOMS

If you love plum blossoms, put these festivals on your itinerary:

* Atami Plum Blossom Festival, from January to March
* Mito Plum Blossom Festival, from late February to late March.

OUTER TOKYO

The beauty of Tokyo's outskirts lies in the seamless transition – the way the city's pulse fades almost imperceptibly into the hush of cedar forests, temples, gardens and river valleys. Within an hour or two, sometimes less, the skyline dissolves into mountains, forests and small, peaceful stations, into places of stillness, history and learning. On central Tokyo's borders, you'll find moss-draped shrines, ornate temples, retro towns, sake breweries and nostalgic trails where birdsong replaces the sound of modernity. You can wander through forests full of childlike whimsy, see cutting-edge architecture, marvel at perfectly formed bonsai or sip tea beside rivers lined with maple and plum trees.

Part of the magic is in the journey itself – fast trains, sleepy locals, the moment glass and steel give way to green. With your Suica or Japan Rail pass in hand, each day trip becomes a rediscovery of Japan's gentle edges. You'll easily return to Tokyo in time for dinner, yet carry with you the scent of mountain air, the echo of temple bells and the calm of having stepped, however briefly, beyond the city's chaotic veil.

MOUNT TAKAO, P 52

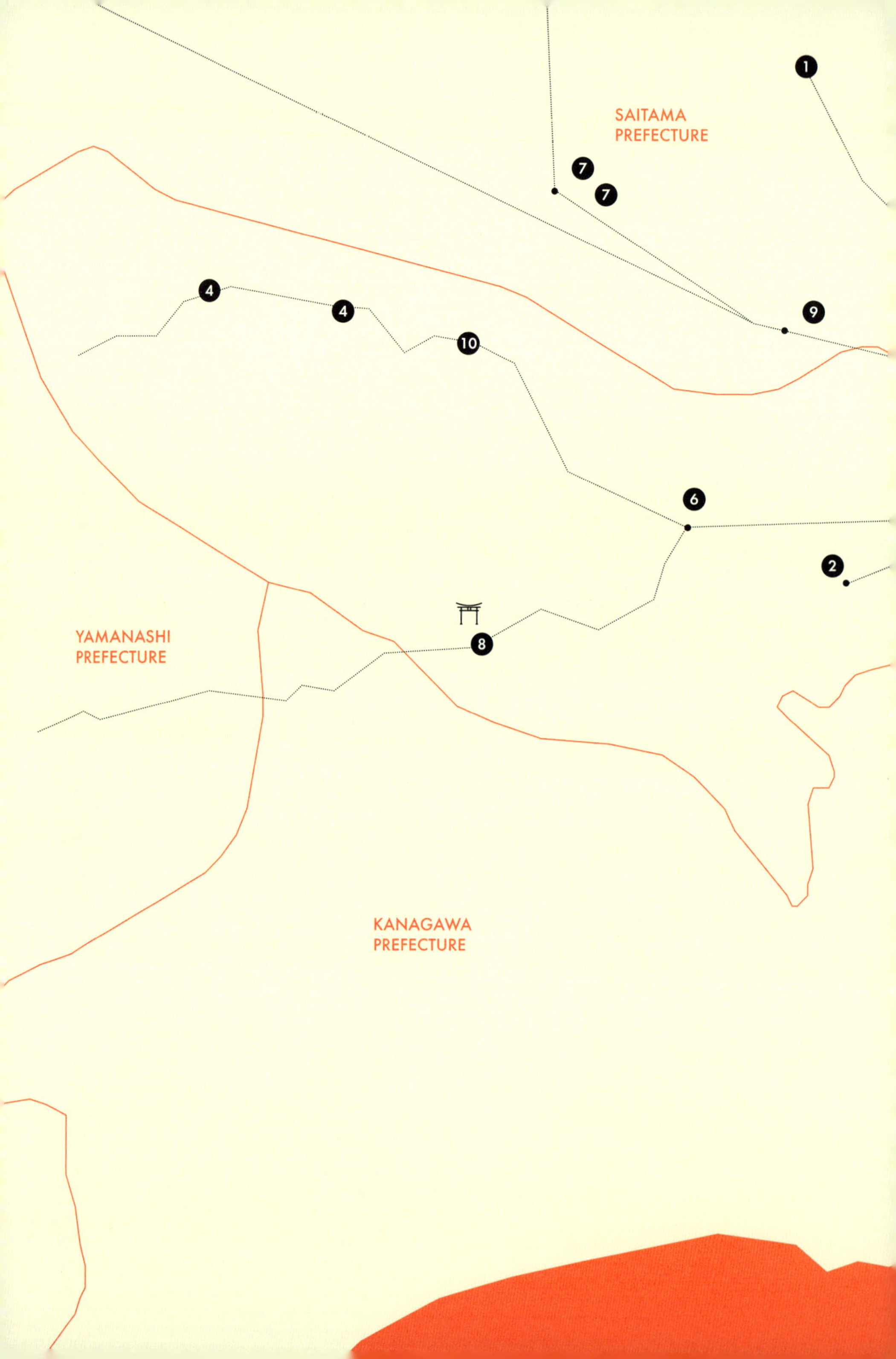

1
SAITAMA
PREFECTURE
7
7
9
4
4
10
6
2
YAMANASHI
PREFECTURE
8
KANAGAWA
PREFECTURE

OUTER TOKYO DAY TRIPS

1. Little Edo in Kawagoe
2. Spiritual Chofu
3. Omiya Bonsai Art Museum & Village
4. Gentle Okutama
5. Nostalgic Shibamata
6. Showa Kinen Park
7. Moomin Worlds
8. Hiking Mount Takao
9. The Kadokawa Musashino Museum
10. Retro Ome
11. Samurai Echoes in Matsudo

KEY

- A Tokyo
- B Narita Airport
- C Haneda Airport
- Shinkansen Routes
- Local Train Routes

Overnighter & Weekender Ideas

→ Okutama

LITTLE EDO IN KAWAGOE

A street lined with Edo-period architecture and a retro sweets alley

30 min

OR

55 min

+

10–15 min

GETTING THERE

From Ikebukuro Station, take the Tobu Tojo Line to Kawagoe Station (30 min). Take the east exit. Or from Seibu-Shinjuku Station, take the Seibu-Shinjuku Line to Hon-Kawagoe Station (55 min). Take the west exit. Follow the signs towards Ichibangai Street from Hon-Kawagoe Station.

koedo.or.jp

DISCOVER

Ichibangai Street, Osawa Family House, Kashiya Yokocho, Toki no Kane, Kita-in Temple.

SEASONAL HIGHLIGHTS

Spring: blossoming cherry trees. Autumn: crisp air, golden light.

Advice → *Visit early morning or twilight for fewer crowds. Rent a kimono for the day to fully immerse yourself in Edo culture – there are several rental shops near the station.*

Kawagoe, affectionately called Little Edo, is a living echo of Tokyo's feudal past – a town of clay-walled kurazukuri warehouses, merchant houses and the faint chime of history ringing in every tiled roof and cobbled path. Once a thriving Edo-period trading hub, it now offers a rare glimpse into the world of samurai and silk merchants.

From **Kawagoe Station**, a gentle walk north leads to **Ichibangai Street**, where the blackened clay facades of old storehouses line the road. Some are centuries old, their beams weathered smooth by time. Within them, shopkeepers sell pottery, lacquerware and simple street food – sweet potatoes, crisp senbei and soft, skewered dango. The **Osawa Family House**, built in 1792, stands as the oldest survivor – a symbol of perseverance and endeavour.

Venture deeper and the scent of caramel and smoke will guide you to **Kashiya Yokocho**, or Candy Alley. Narrow and cobblestoned, it glimmers with glass bottles of ramune soda and trays of candied yams. Once a centre of sweet-making for Edo's merchants, this street is now one of Japan's officially recognised 'Top 100 Fragrant Landscapes'.

The **Toki no Kane** – Kawagoe's 'Bell of Time' – has marked the hours for centuries. The original tower was destroyed in the 1650s; its current three-tiered wooden form was rebuilt in 1894 after the Great Fire of 1893, which destroyed a third of Kawagoe's buildings. Four times a day – 6 am, noon, 3 pm and 6 pm – its warm chime drifts across rooftops, a sound so beloved it's counted among Japan's '100 Soundscapes'. Even now, locals still use it to tell the time.

A short walk away, **Kawagoe Hikawa Shrine** has been a place of love and matchmaking since ancient times – perhaps as far back as the 6th century. In summer, thousands of glass furin wind chimes tinkle in the breeze, carrying whispered prayers for romance.

Little remains of **Kawagoe Castle**, yet what survives is precious. In the 1600s, Tokugawa Iemitsu – a shogun who adored Kawagoe – moved parts of **Edo Castle** here. When the Great Kanto Earthquake later levelled much of Edo in 1923, these structures endured, becoming rare surviving fragments of the shogunate's heart. Nearby, the **Kita-in Temple** preserves this legacy. Within its quiet grounds stand the **Gohyaku Rakan** – 540 stone disciples of Buddha – and the **Honmaru Goten**, a palace hall once part of the original castle.

End your walk by enjoying a meal of the town's famous unagi don, eel grilled to perfection and brushed with a secret sauce.

SPIRITUAL CHOFU

A whisper of the old city, where cedar, cinema and myth entwine

30 min

15 min

OR

30 min

GETTING THERE

From Shinjuku Station, take the Keio Line to Chofu Station (30 min). Take the north exit and catch the Chofu 34 bus (15 min) or walk (30 min) to Jindai-ji Temple.

city.chofu.lg.jp

DISCOVER

Jindai-ji Temple, Jindai Botanical Gardens, Sengawa Theatre, Toei Studios, Kitaro Chaya cafe, Yumori no Sato onsen.

SEASONAL HIGHLIGHTS

Spring: plum blossoms, rose season. Autumn: maples.

Advice → *Bring small coins for temple bells – and time enough to get lost among the cedars.*

Only 30 minutes from Shinjuku's neon rush, **Chofu** feels like another world – slower, greener, quietly enchanted. You'll watch from the window as the train glides past tower blocks into tree-lined calm, where the air hums with cicadas and the edges of Tokyo blur into memory.

By late morning, sunlight filters through the cedars as you wander towards **Jindai-ji Temple**, Tokyo's second-oldest. Founded in the 8th century, this Tendai Sect temple feels hidden from time. Moss softens its stone steps, plum blossoms scatter across the paths and incense curls upwards in faint spirals. The main gate, rebuilt in 1695, opens onto halls that shelter the **Hakuho Buddha** – Eastern Japan's oldest seated statue. A bell from 1376 still marks the hours, its sacred tone resonating through the grove. Twice a day, at 11 am and 2 pm, you can participate in daily prayers (for a fee). The Goma Fire Ritual is part of the ceremony.

Beside the temple, the **Jindai Botanical Gardens** stretch wide and serene. In spring, the rose garden blooms in a riot of colour and scent; summer brings the cool shade of hydrangeas; autumn burns in maple red. Dragonflies skim the ponds, couples rest on benches, and you'll find time slowing to the rhythm of rustling trees.

But Chofu is not just stillness. It's a town alive with stories – both mythic and cinematic. At the **Sengawa Theatre**, the raw concrete form of Tadao Ando's building rises amid green, a hymn to creativity. From here, explore nearby **Toei Studios**, which continues Chofu's long romance with film, producing samurai dramas, love stories and the beloved hero Kamen Rider.

Anime fans will trace the spirit of Shigeru Mizuki's yokai (supernatural beings in Japanese folklore) through **Tenjin Dori**, a shopping street where you can find **Kitaro Chaya**, a cafe based on Mizuki's series *GeGeGe no Kitaro*. Inside, enjoy playful, character-themed dishes and exclusive memorabilia.

On **Jindaiji-dori**, stop for handmade soba, Chofu's signature dish; its buckwheat is grown nearby – even schoolchildren help cultivate it for the Botanical Gardens' kitchen. Then it's time to linger longer, and soak beneath trees at **Yumori no Sato**, a rustic onsen with milky-white waters and a treehouse bath, where the city's static finally fades.

Chofu is Tokyo's exhale – a place where faith, folklore and film meet the forest, and where, for a few hours, you will remember how to breathe.

青木屋伝統
二八蕎麦
青木屋伝統
二八蕎麦

OMIYA BONSAI ART MUSEUM & VILLAGE

Timeless and gentle town with bonsai on display everywhere

Train	30 min
OR		
Train	30 min
+		
Walk	10 min

GETTING THERE

From Tokyo Station, take the Tobu Urban Park Line to Omiya-koen Station. Or from Shinjuku Station, take the Shonan Shinjuku Line to Omiya Station (both 30 min). Take the west exit and follow the signs to the Bonsai Village.

bonsai-art-museum.jp

DISCOVER

Mansei-en, Seiko-en, Fuyo-en, Toju-en, Omiya Bonsai Art Museum.

SEASONAL HIGHLIGHTS

Spring: Bonsai Festival (May), when flowering bonsai are beginning to bud. Summer: main season for trimming. Autumn: fiery colours on maple and ginkgo bonsai. Winter: skeletal shapes of tiny trees.

Advice → *If you have a JR Pass that includes the Tokyo Wide Pass, take the Tohoku Shinkansen from Tokyo Station to Omiya Station in just 25 minutes.*

Bring cash for nursery entry fees and allow enough time – bonsai reward the unhurried eye.

Omiya is also known for the Hikawa Shrine and Omiya udon, usually served cold with a dipping sauce.

Leaving Tokyo's restlessness behind, you'll step from the train station and enter a quieter dimension – one shaped by reverence and patience. Here, in **Omiya Bonsai Village**, time moves slowly, bending like a branch under a careful hand. The air is fragrant with pine and earth, thick with tradition and history.

This enclave of mastery was born from disaster. After the Great Kanto Earthquake of 1923, Tokyo's bonsai artisans fled the ruined city and replanted their lives here in **Omiya**, creating a living community of miniature worlds. A century later, their legacy endures in narrow streets lined with nurseries – **Mansei-en**, **Seiko-en**, **Toju-en**, **Fuyo-en** – each a studio of quiet concentration where trees are trained, shaped and entrusted to the future.

In these gardens, devotion is measured in millimetres and decades. A master may never see the full grace of the tree they begin, yet they shape it tenderly, knowing the work will be completed by unseen hands. Watching them, scissors glinting in morning light, you'll feel time and knowledge take root.

At the **Omiya Bonsai Art Museum**, the philosophy unfolds in perfect miniature. In the open-air garden, trees rise from raked gravel – gnarled pines, maples poised in eternal spring, cypress bowed with age. From the balcony above, the scene resembles a dream of nature compressed and refined. The museum's treasure, a 500-year-old white pine, presides over all – a living sculpture, a grand old monarch.

Inside, the museum offers the tools of the craft – shears, wires, elegant pots and books – invitations to begin your own lifelong study of bonsai. Some nurseries welcome visitors to workshops: at Mansei-en, bonsai lessons have been offered since the Edo period; at Seiko-en, master Hiroshi Ishihara guides beginners through the art of bonsai in English, his words as gentle as the subtle art of pruning itself. If you're keen, workshops must be booked ahead.

By afternoon's end, you'll likely look at the world differently – as though every tree holds a tiny secret, every seed a possibility.

GENTLE OKUTAMA

A peaceful area for hikes, waterfalls and renowned sake

80 min

40 min

GETTING THERE

From Shinjuku Station, take the JR Chuo Line to Ome, then transfer to the Ome Line for Okutama Station (2 hr). Take the main exit and follow signs for the hiking trails.

Alternatively, get off at at Mitake Station for Mitake Gorge or Sawai Station for Sawanoi Ozawa Brewery.

okutama.gr.jp

DISCOVER

Hyakuhiro Falls, Hossawa Falls, Lake Okutama, Nippara Limestone Caves, Sawanoi Ozawa Brewery.

SEASONAL HIGHLIGHTS

Spring: fresh green foliage.
Summer: riverside walks.
Autumn: stunning maples.

Overnighter → *Stay overnight or at a base camp to explore fully. Wear good shoes; trails can be slippery.*

West of Tokyo's restless energy, the JR Chuo Line carries passengers towards stillness. Towers give way to tiled rooftops, and as the train arrives at Ome Station for the change to the Ome Line, the rhythm of the city slows down. The train hugs the Tama River, sunlight flickering through the glass, until it arrives at Okutama Station – a final frontier of green. The air here is sharp and clean and the sky seems to widen above the mountains.

A short bus ride to **Kawanoribashi** marks the beginning of a pilgrimage into nature's quiet heart. The trail to **Hyakuhiro Falls** climbs beside the **Kawakoketani River**, where water ribbons over moss and smooth rock. The climb can test the legs, but rewards the soul: the falls are a 40-metre (131-foot) curtain of silver spilling into a jade pool, framed by forest and the perfume of wet earth.

Okutama is a land of water. **Hossawa Falls**, among Japan's 'Top 100 Waterfalls', plunges 60 metres (197 feet), breaking into four tiers that sparkle like spun glass. Local legend warns of a serpent spirit sleeping in the pool below – a reminder that even paradise has its guardians. Other recommended falls are **Ayahiro Falls** and **Mitsugama Falls**, a three-pool waterfall just a 1.5-kilometre (0.9-mile) hike from Okutama Station.

If hiking seems too taxing, there are other good reasons to visit Okutama. Alight at Mitake Station, where you'll find the deep and picturesque ravine **Mitake Gorge**. One stop along, **Sawanoi Ozawa Brewery** at Sawai Station finds mountain air mingling with the fragrance of fermenting rice. Taste sake born from pure river water and watch the light fade through the trees. Take a tour of the factory, a fascinating lesson in centuries of sake production. The brewery expands across the road to **Seiryu Garden Sawanoi-en**, a riverside dining haven where you can partake in sake tastings, buy the brewery's sake and enjoy sake-flavoured soft-serve. As an added bonus, the charming **Kanzanji Temple** (founded in 1930 by calligrapher Taguchi Beiho) is perched on the opposite bank.

For the return to Tokyo, at the station pick up an ekiben highlighting the local specialties – grilled trout with miso or mountain vegetables on rice – and maybe a jar of Okutama honey, a sweet reminder of a perfect day.

澤乃井
奥多摩湧水仕込
澤乃井
清酒
大吟醸
澤乃井
TOKYO JAPAN
特別純米
澤乃井
本地酒
澤乃井
本地酒

ドアに引き込まれないようにご注意ください
ドアにてをつかないでね！
青梅鉄道公園

NOSTALGIC SHIBAMATA

Part temple town, part Showa daydream – a riverside remnant of old Tokyo

25 min

11 min

GETTING THERE

From Ueno Station, take the Keisei Line to Keisei Takasago Station, then transfer to the Keisei Kanamachi Line to Shibamata Station (35–40 min). Take the main exit; statues of Tora-san and Sakura mark the start of Taishakuten Sando.

shibamata.net

DISCOVER

Taishakuten Sando, Shibamata Taishakuten Temple, Edogawa Riverside.

SEASONAL HIGHLIGHTS

Spring: cherry blossoms by the river. Summer: fireworks festivals, lush greenery. Autumn: temple maples in crimson hues.

Advice → *Try kusa dango fresh off the grill. Combine your visit with Katsushika Shibamata Tora-san Museum for Showa-era nostalgia.*

Shibamata is Tokyo's memory – a place where the artisan and the people forge an intense, spiritual understanding. It can be found on Tokyo's northeastern edge, as the city sprawl fans out into rivers and parks. The neighbourhood is full of charm and feels as if it has barely changed in a century. Lanterns still sway over narrow streets and long-standing shops still run by their original families spill with rice crackers and sweet dango. Here, history lives in every wooden eave, every classic frontage and every shopkeeper's smile.

Shibamata is known for the popular movie series *Otoko wa Tsurai yo* (*It's Tough Being a Man*), and you'll see brass statues of the beloved central characters Tora-san and Sakura in front of the station.

The shopping street **Taishakuten Sando** buzzes with life and yet retains a breezy, weekend feel, a respite from the fast pace of Tokyo. The popular street snack here is kusa dango, green with mugwort, skewered three at a time, shiny with sweet soy glaze. Toy shop windows tell a story of yesterday, of quality and service, displaying tin wind-up cars and spinning tops. Geta sandals clatter on the cobbles, mixing with the lively chatter of locals who seem to have been plucked from a Miyazaki animation.

Taishakuten Sando leads up to **Shibamata Taishakuten Temple**, its wooden gates famous for their intricate carvings of dragons, flowers and rolling waves. The temple garden is a miniature world, where koi circle slowly in ponds with gently running water. Over 500 years old, the temple carvings are legendary and were worked upon by the same artist who carved the astounding gates at Nikko's Toshogu Shrine (see page 77). In front of the main hall, a large pine tree takes the shape of a fierce guardian dragon. The panels at the back of the **Taishakudo Hall**, the temple's wooden prayer hall, are a must-see – extraordinarily detailed and unchanged, art and spirituality as one, seemingly unaffected by time.

From the temple, wander towards the banks of the **Edogawa River**. Here, old ferry boats once moved people and goods between provinces. Today, it's Tokyo's last remaining boat crossing, where visitors can drift down the river as if carrying their own cargo. In summer, fireworks burst in the sky high above the river and spray colour across the surface of the water.

SHOWA KINEN PARK

Expansive and seasonal – suburban Tokyo's breathing space

~30 min (train)

10–15 min (walk)

GETTING THERE

From Shinjuku Station, take the JR Chuo Line to Tachikawa Station (~30 min). Park entrances are a 10–15-minute walk from the station's main exit. Bicycle rentals are available inside the park.

showakinen-koen.jp

DISCOVER

Japanese Garden, Ginkgo Avenue, Flowering Tree Garden, Komorebi Village, Waterfowl Pond, Nemophila Garden.

SEASONAL HIGHLIGHTS

Spring: cherry blossoms, tulips. Summer: lotus blooms. Autumn: cosmos, Ginkgo Avenue in radiant colour. Winter: crisp stillness, night illuminations.

Advice → *Rent a bicycle to cover the park's vastness; bring a picnic and stay for the seasonal night illuminations in late autumn and winter.*

Beyond Tokyo's thrum, **Showa Kinen Park** is a vast, breathing world that inhabits an otherwise normal part of outer suburban Tokyo. Opened in 1983 to mark Emperor Hirohito's 50th year on the throne, this 180-hectare (445-acre) expanse isn't merely a park; it's a shifting calendar of the seasons, a place where the year turns its own luminous pages.

The area around **Tachikawa** feels wider, looser and unusually suburban by Tokyo standards: cyclists gliding; families wheeling prams; and broad avenues, bypasses and thoroughfares. However, enter the park through **Tachikawa Gate** or **Nishi-Tachikawa Gate**, and the day suddenly blooms.

Rent a bike once you're in the park – around ¥800 for the day – to comfortably explore its vast grounds. Pedal beneath zelkova and ginkgo canopies, their branches sketching shifting patterns of shade, as if the park is quietly introducing itself in chapters rather than sights, every season rewriting the park's story. Spring blushes with cherry trees and tulips, and the soft blue haze of the **Nemophila Garden** is a pool of colour. Summer drifts by on lotus ponds and paddle boats; autumn arrives with the full theatre of cosmos and flame-bright maples.

In autumn **Ginkgo Avenue** transforms into a vaulted cathedral of molten gold, leaves falling to create a faded yellow walkway. There are three ways to wander here – by foot, by bike or aboard the cheerful yellow park train that loops around ponds and meadows, its windows filled with waving children. Explore the **Komorebi Village**, with its thatched houses telling tales of farm life and firewood, of a pace many of us have long forgotten. Children run off, laughing, into their own realms – the Bouncing Dome, the Mist Forest, the Rainbow Hammocks – small universes of joy. This park is perfect for families, for play, for strolling, for discovery.

Showa Kinen is a park, but it's also a conversation, an exchange between people and nature. It's a place that changes you as you move through it – a reminder that time, like a leaf, is most beautiful when it drifts.

MOOMIN WORLDS

The fairytale forest glade of Akebono Park and the lakeside landscape of Moomin Valley Park

50–60 min

20 min

10 min

GETTING THERE

From Ikebukuro Station, take the Seibu Ikebukuro Line to Hanno Station (50–60 min). Akebono Children's Forest Park is 20 minutes by taxi/bus and Moomin Valley Park is 10 minutes by shuttle bus from Hanno Station's north exit.

Akebono Park: city.hanno.lg.jp
Moomin Valley Park: metsa-hanno.com

DISCOVER

Akebono Park: mushroom houses, spiral towers, forest ponds.

Moomin Valley Park: Moominhouse, Lake Miyazawa, story hall, Nordic cafes.

SEASONAL HIGHLIGHTS

Spring: blossoms and fresh leaves at both parks. Summer: shaded forest in Akebono Park; bright lakeside trails in Moomin Valley Park. Autumn: golden foliage framing fairy houses and the lake. Winter: snow-dusted, quiet, fairytale landscapes.

Advice → *If you fancy an onsen after visiting Moomin Valley Park, immerse yourself in nearby superb public bath Kirari.*

About an hour from Tokyo, in the wooded glades of **Saitama Prefecture**, adorable folktales come to life. Two areas pay homage to Tove Jansson's Moomins – gentle, philosophical creatures from Finland. Together, **Tove Jansson Akebono Children's Forest Park** and **Moomin Valley Park** create a twin pilgrimage into story, nature and the lingering presence of childhood.

Step first into Akebono Park, hidden among cedars and streams, where organic buildings curve like mushrooms and staircases spiral up into towers that seem to grow from the earth. Moss thatches roofs, ivy curls over doors, and wooden bridges span gently gurgling waters. Park benches are a conduit for Moomin tales, and mystical houses come slowly into view behind green hills as you turn corners. The air is alive with scent – especially in spring, when wildflowers paint the park. It feels more like a dreamscape than a theme park: part Finnish fairytale, part Japanese whimsy. A cafe and a small museum dedicated to Jansson are open during daylight hours.

About 4 kilometres (2.5 miles) to the north of Akebono you'll find Moomin Valley Park spread out along the edge of **Lake Miyazawa**. Rising above the still waters is **Moominhouse**, with its blue tower and crooked staircases. Its rooms include Moominmamma's kitchen and Snufkin's corner, looking as if the classic characters have momentarily stepped out for a walk. In a series of spots around the picturesque lake you'll find trails, bridges, a story hall with Jansson's illustrations, a Moomin-themed play area (the quirky and off-kilter **Hemuli's Playground**), cafes and a stage where Moomin tales are brought to life in energetic shows. It's like wandering into a living story book where you become an honorary Moomin. As night descends, the spell deepens: lanterns glow, stillness settles on the valley and the peaceful Moomin way of life seeps into every corner.

Both parks embody the wistful gentleness of Tove Jansson's work, and both provide a landscape of dreams, where play mingles with imagination and nature – yet they are different in atmosphere. To visit both parks in a single day is to experience two halves of the same story.

HIKING MOUNT TAKAO

Accessible hikes with stunning views on a sacred mountain

50 min

GETTING THERE

From Shinjuku Station, take the Keio Line to Takaosanguchi Station (50 min). The station sits at the base of the mountain. Cable car and chairlift stations are a short walk from the main exit.

Trails: Route 1 (main, paved, via Yakuo-in Temple); Route 6 (forest and streamside); Inariyama Trail (ridge route, views); other routes link to deeper ranges, such as Mount Jimba.

takaosan.or.jp

DISCOVER

Hikes, Yakuo-in Temple with Tengu guardians, cable car and chairlift, summit views towards Mount Fuji, teahouses for soba, dango and mountain snacks.

SEASONAL HIGHLIGHTS

Spring: cherry blossoms, wildflowers. Summer: cooling shade. Autumn: luminous maples. Winter: stark bare trees against crisp skies, distant Mount Fuji at its most visible.

Advice → *Although manageable, it's still a hike, so remember: good boots and plenty of water. After the rigours of hiking, soak away aches and pains at Keio Takaosan Onsen Gokurakuyu, a contemporary yet atmospheric bathhouse right behind the station.*

Less than an hour from Shinjuku, **Mount Takao** is a perfect day hike along the ridge of a verdant mountain with spectacular views of the surrounding landscape. Cedars, shrines and birdsong await. Monks have walked these trails in devotion for centuries; today, hikers, pilgrims and nature lovers follow in their footsteps, treading the very path that the Tengu Spirit walks. It's a perfect scenario – an easy jaunt from the big city to a mountain with a 599-metre (1965-feet) elevation. It seems remote and deeply tranquil. The only reminder that you are less than an hour away from Tokyo is the spectacular sight of the not-too-distant metropolis on the horizon.

First, stop to admire Takaosanguchi Station, architect Kengo Kuma's spiritual homage to nearby **Yakuo-in Temple**, which makes excellent use of the area's majestic cedars. From here it isn't far to the cable car, the steepest in Japan, and its companion chairlift. Pick a mode of transport and climb aboard to be transported to a higher plane, Takao's midway slope. There are six main walking trails on Takao, plus the ridge-top **Inariyama Trail**, each a different way of experiencing the moods of the mountain and each with a different degree of difficulty. The most popular, **Route 1**, is wide, partially paved and an easy level for seasoned hikers and not too taxing for the casual mountain stroller. Walk past magnificent trees, views, sacred sites and the peaceful Yakuo-in Temple, which was established in 744 CE. Its red torii gates and Tengu guardian statues lead to the spiritual sanctuary of the Shugendo priests, who practise mountain asceticism. Prayers, bells and the soft scent of cedar give the temple grounds a special ambience. From the mountain's ridge on clear days, **Mount Fuji** is a distant deity.

For those seeking nature's hush, **Route 6** follows a stream into a cool, mossy forest. In summer it is a shaded refuge, while in autumn the red and yellow leaves form colourful canopies. Though slightly more rigorous than Route 1, the trail is only 3.3 kilometres (2 miles) long, with a completion time of around 2.5 hours. It's here you'll find the famed **Biwataki Waterfall**, where the ascetic monks perform their practices, including meditating directly under the cascading water.

THE KADOKAWA MUSASHINO MUSEUM

A futuristic, sensory library made of granite

Train	30 min
Train	10 min
Walk	10 min

GETTING THERE
From Ikebukuro Station, take the Seibu Ikebukuro Line to Tokorozawa Station (30 min), then transfer to the Seibu Sayama Line to Higashi-Tokorozawa Station (10 min). The museum is a 10-minute walk from the station's west exit.

kadcul.com

DISCOVER
Bookshelf Theater and Edit Town – Book Street; rotating art, anime and manga exhibitions; Kengo Kuma architecture, both exterior granite shell and sculptural interiors; surrounding Tokorozawa Sakura Town.

SEASONAL HIGHLIGHTS
All seasons, as exhibitions change frequently.

Advice → *Evening visits are recommended for the Bookshelf Theater projection mapping. For children and anime lovers, the museum connects seamlessly to the larger Tokorozawa Sakura Town, where there are souvenir shops, cafes, a capsule toy studio and spaces that celebrate Japanese pop culture.*

We love to travel for a lesser-known, outstanding piece of architecture. The skill, patience and sheer audacity of constructing eye-popping, potentially unhinged mega-structures in out-of-the-way places always appeal to our sense of discovery. So we can highly recommend **Tokorozawa Sakura Town**, a pop-culture hub set in a tranquil, green and unassuming area, because it's here that the **Kadokawa Musashino Museum** rises from the land like a monolithic, prehistoric flower. Architect Kengo Kuma's granite ark is clad in an astounding 20,000 slabs of grey stone – a futuristic boulder-spacecraft hybrid that hides an immersive library. It is a sacred temple to words and images, a place where you'll feel like literature, manga, anime and art have been dwelling since the dawn of time.

Inside, the **Bookshelf Theater** will take your breath away: an atrium soaring 8 metres (26 feet) high, lined with towering shelves stacked with 20,000 books. The tomes are piled high, an ocean of spines – encyclopedias, art monographs, literature – teetering and crooked and seeming to disappear into the high ceiling as if you're standing in a mystical library at Hogwarts. Every 20 minutes, digital projection mapping transforms the shelves into a narrative, a filmic immersion of light and experimental sound, transporting you into a world of language and story.

The structure also houses multiple galleries, with exhibitions ranging from contemporary art to manga and anime, and **Edit Town**'s 'city of books' will amaze you with its cultural archives and its relaxing spaces allowing you to read, absorb and lose yourself among the many works. There's definitely a sense of sci-fi and fantasy – you might find Studio Ghibli sketches beside digital installations, or themed exhibitions that dive deep into the more creative and visual side of gaming. To us, the building itself felt like an exhibit: stone walls set at slanted angles, light streaming in, part sacred, part playful, part cinematic.

The museum's grounds also feature the **Musashino Reiwa Shrine**, a startling contemporary structure complete with steel tori tunnel and tori gate.

The architecture is solemn, the anime and pop-culture references playful – Japan's cultural DNA in ancient, monolithic halls, bound together under granite, majesty and holy light.

RETRO OME

月形龍之介・中村錦之助
東千代之介・里見浩太郎・丘さとみ
水戸黄門
天下の副将軍
監督・松田定次
東映スコープ
総天然色
脚本・菊島隆三
黒沢明
黒沢明監督
用心棒
三船敏郎
仲代達矢
千両獅子
市川右太衛門
明日大公開
大人 80円
60円
映画看板にはお手をふれないようお願いします！！

A delightful town happily stuck in the 20th century

~75 min

GETTING THERE

From Shinjuku Station, take the JR Chuo Line to Ome Station (~75 min). Take the main exit.

omekanko.gr.jp

DISCOVER

Retro signboards and film billboards by Seizo Tajima, Showa Retro Packaging Museum, Ome Kimono Museum, Tama River for swimming or picnics.

SEASONAL HIGHLIGHTS

Spring: riverbanks in bloom, cherry blossoms along the Tama River. Summer: clear river swims, mountain hikes. Autumn: golden leaves in surrounding hills. Winter: quiet streets, Ome Daruma Market (January).

Advice → *In January, the Ome Daruma Market fills the streets with stalls selling bright red daruma dolls, their white eyes waiting to be painted with wishes.*

An hour west of Shinjuku, where the city begins to melt into hills and forests, you'll find **Ome**, a town that happily forgot to leave the 20th century. If you love anything vintage, there's something about late Showa-era Japan from the 1950s to the 1980s that's so alluring. It's the birth of pop culture: sturdy toys, inventive ideas, crazy characters, colourful graphics – they all speak of a time when the world was changing and pop was an emerging force. Ome embodies this with a retro charm. It's a place where nostalgia isn't staged – it's lived.

Showa-era storefronts still line the streets, with their wooden facades, charming signage and mom-and-pop eateries serving curry rice and handmade manju. Hand-painted billboards for classic or long-forgotten films crack and peel on crumbling walls: cowboys at full gallop, other-worldly geisha, samurai ready for battle. Local artist Seizo Tajima painted many of these retro billboards, and the town feels like a living museum, exhibiting his extensive and celebrated work. Walking among them is like drifting into an old Japanese cinematic reel. Ome Station is the perfect welcome, adorned with its own towering billboards for classic movies (take note of the station departure melody; it's the theme from popular anime *The Secret of Akko-Chan*).

Museums exhibit the vintage legacy proudly. The **Ome Kimono Museum** and the **Showa Retro Packaging Museum** preserve fragments of mid-20th-century life: candy tins, matchboxes, patterned yukata, magazine covers, movie advertising, cigarette packaging – everyday ephemera now exhibits of memory and nostalgia. Snacks from the time make it more authentic, with retro sweets and drinks in bottles and boxes with colourful graphics.

Although this makes Ome seem like one big sentimental theme park, the town also seamlessly blends the nostalgic with the natural. Minutes away from the storefronts and exhibitions you'll find yourself beside the **Tama River**, the air smelling of waterweed and stone. In summer, children splash in its shallows and try to net minnows. Families spread blankets for picnics, and couples dangle bare feet from low bridges. In spring, cherry blossoms scatter across the water, petals twirling downstream like small pink fairy boats. In autumn, the river reflects luminous maples. Trails lead into hills dotted with temples and impressive vistas.

It's Tokyo's contrasting nature in one perfect stop.

SAMURAI ECHOES IN MATSUDO

A town with a rich samurai past and historic estate

~25 min

GETTING THERE

From Tokyo Station, take the JR Joban Line to Matsudo Station (~25 min). Take the east exit.

city.matsudo.chiba.jp

DISCOVER

Tojo-tei estate (samurai house and garden of the last Mito clan lord), historic roads of the Mito Kaido, old samurai ranchlands and horse pastures of the Tokugawa era in Kogane area.

SEASONAL HIGHLIGHTS

Early spring: plum blossoms in Tojo-tei garden. Autumn: maple leaves, quiet streets. Late winter: plum blossoms.

Advice → *Many sites are near the station so you can explore on foot. Bring comfortable shoes and allow at least half a day. Visit on weekday mornings for fewer crowds and a gentler pace.*

Within easy reach of Tokyo, **Matsudo** is an atmospheric town that shows a quieter side of Japan's samurai past. The city lies where the old Mito Kaido (historic road) branched off from Edo, where post towns were built for foot-sore travellers and to rest and water the warhorses owned by the shogunate.

Not far from the east exit of Matsudo Station is the **Tojo-tei estate**. Built in 1884 for Tokugawa Akitake – younger brother of the last shogun – the estate is surrounded by the verdant expanse of **Tojogaoka Historical Park**. Shoji screen doors open to a seasonal garden of plum, ginkgo and moss. Inside, tatami mats and wooden walkways guide you to rooms that place you inside the life of the samurai. Light falls beautifully through the screens onto small alcove shrines and pale wooden beams, while thin walkways are framed by glass sliding doors, affording views of small water gardens. The bathroom is a delight, the tiled soaking bath providing a glimpse of what weary samurai could look forward to after travel. On the edge of the park, the small **Tojo Museum of History** exhibits items from the era.

Nearby, the **Edogawa River**, along which goods once floated into the city, now flows quietly, memories of history and trade carried on ghostly barges.

It's easy to forget that while shogun and samurai roamed the land, horses were in great demand, an essential tool of the Meiji era. To the southeast in the **Kogane-maki pastures**, where wild stallions were once gathered for cavalry, you can almost hear the proud whinnies of horses calling across the grassland.

To cap off a perfect day, pop in to **Ramen Tomita**, the flagship store for the award-winning ramen restaurant, regarded as Japan's number one. Osamu Tomita, featured in the documentary *Ramen Heads*, mastered his tsukumen here. The tiny, atmospheric corner eatery serves superb noodles and broth. Order from a ticket machine in the doorway and then expect to queue for an hour or more depending on what time and day you go. Steve's tip? Get the tokusei tsukesoba.

As twilight approaches, the lanterns of the Tojo-tei garden begin to glow, and the spirit of the Meiji era seems to return to Matsudo's streets. Sip matcha under plum trees, enjoying the peace. Matsudo rarely appears in travel books or bloggers' top ten lists, yet here in the quiet fold of the suburbs, the edges of an era can be traced: when bamboo fences marked boundaries of clan and land, when roads echoed with the drumming canter of warhorses or the gentle whisper of travellers' prayers.

GHIBLI PILGRIMAGES: FORESTS, GARDENS & DREAMSCAPES

Scattered through forests, suburbs and former exposition grounds are real places that quietly shaped Studio Ghibli co-founder Hayao Miyazaki's imagination. These day trips reward unhurried travellers – those willing to let the boundary between animation and reality gently blur. Before the soundtracks swell and the credits roll, there is another way into Miyazaki's world. It begins on foot. Follow Mei as she disappears down a narrow forest path, Catbus just ahead, blinking through the trees. Join Totoro and pause the day with a nap beneath camphor leaves, while soot sprites scatter across the floorboards of an old farmhouse. These journeys are not about spectacle, but about immersion: listening to the wind in the grass, to cicadas humming like a held note; strolling through neighbourhood gardens that shaped extraordinary stories. From the mossy folds of Sayama Hills to the unassuming lanes of Asagaya, and onwards to a park where imagination has taken physical form, think of these places as Ghibli scenes without a script: you arrive, you wander and you find that something small and magical.

DAY TRIP: TOTORO'S FOREST NO. 1

North of Tokyo, the **Sayama Hills** roll softly across the border of Saitama and Tokyo, a rare pocket of Satoyama landscape – traditional countryside where woodlands, fields and village life overlap. This is the place widely known as **Totoro's Forest**, a mosaic of preserved green spaces that inspired *My Neighbor Totoro*.

The walk is gentle and contemplative: dirt paths beneath tall trees, filtered light, birdsong and the occasional glimpse of suburban rooftops beyond the forest edge. At the heart of the forest is **Kurosuke's House**, a restored early Showa-era farmhouse where Totoro himself might just be napping, waiting behind shoji screens. Inside, displays explain local conservation efforts and Miyazaki's connection to the area. This is not a theme park – it's an act of preservation, Totoro's wishes realised, the deeper magic of the forest. Allow half a day to wander slowly, breathe deeply and awaken the spirit of Totoro inside yourself.

10 am–3 pm (Tue, Wed, Sat); apply in advance to visit: www.totoro.or.jp/kurosuke

DAY TRIP: A-SAN NO NIWA & EDO-TOKYO OPEN AIR ARCHITECTURAL MUSEUM

Begin in **Asagaya**, a low-rise, lived-in Tokyo neighbourhood. A short walk from the station brings you to **A-san no Niwa**, meaning A's Garden, where A means 'anyone' or 'visitors' – so it's anyone's, or everyone's, garden. It's a modest but deeply evocative green space. Miyazaki wrote about this garden in *The House Where Totoro Lives*, describing it as a personal refuge and creative touchstone. So much so that he then designed the space to reflect the profound effect it had on his creations. Sadly, the original Totoro House burnt down, but instead you'll find a whimsical and delightful garden with a small cottage, pathways, gates and picket fences that allow you to wander and contemplate Miyazaki's tender inner world.

From Asagaya, return by train towards Musashi-Koganei Station, then continue on foot, by bus or by taxi to the **Edo-Tokyo Open Air Architectural Museum**. This expansive outdoor museum assembles historic buildings from across Tokyo and across time, reconstructed on extensive parklands. Walking through the re-created old Showa-era streetscape of shops, houses and buildings feels uncannily like stepping into a Ghibli background painting. The museum was a major inspiration for Miyazaki, in particular the picturesque old bathhouse, which became part of the blueprint for the bathhouse in *Spirited Away*. Together, A-san no Niwa and the museum form a dialogue between imagination and ordinary life – the domestic worlds that Miyazaki elevated into wonder.

If you have time, or perhaps on another day, no pilgrimage to this softer side of Ghibli is really complete without a visit to the **Ghibli Museum**, tucked away in the leafy calm of neighbourhood Tokyo's **Inokashira Park**. Here, Miyazaki's world turns inward and playful: staircases curl without explanation, stained glass glows with familiar silhouettes and short films flicker like private dreams. There is no fixed path – much like *Spirited Away*, you wander and piece things together for yourself. Outside, the park is a reminder that imagination doesn't end at the exit; it simply slips back into the trees.

Entry to Ghibli Museum is strictly by advance reservation. Tickets go on sale on the tenth day of each month for the following month and often sell out within hours, especially on weekends and during school holidays. Entry is timed, with arrivals staggered every 30 minutes to control crowds, and most visitors spend 2–3 hours inside.

Apply in advance to visit the Ghibli Museum and A-san no Niwa: https://experience-suginami.tokyo/2016/01/a-san-no-niwa; www.tatemonoen.jp; www.ghibli-museum.jp

OVERNIGHT JOURNEY: GHIBLI PARK

Ghibli Park is not a single destination but a constellation of five spaces: Ghibli's Grand Warehouse, Hill of Youth, Dondoko Forest, Mononoke Village and Valley of Witches, languishing in the vast grounds of **Expo 2005 Aichi Commemorative Park**. The atmosphere is more country escape than amusement park. It is a place designed to be walked through, lingered in and quietly absorbed – just like the worlds that inspired it.

This is a day trip that demands planning: tickets are released two months in advance and often sell out immediately. Premium passes allow access to the five spaces; standard tickets cover three. The one-way journey takes just under 3 hours. From Tokyo, take the Nozomi Shinkansen to Nagoya, then connect via the Higashiyama and Linimo lines to Aichikyuhaku-kinen-koen, from where the park is an 8-minute walk. Or take the Meitetsu bus near Nagoya Station straight to the park. While technically doable as a long day trip, Ghibli Park is best savoured as an overnight stay. Travel packages – including transport and accommodation are available.

Apply in advance to visit: www.ghibli-park.jp

NORTH

North of Tokyo, the landscape widens into fertile plains, farm towns and verdant mountains. Vast skies stretch low over wondrous gardens and hiking trails lead deep into forests and across marshes, where steaming hot springs speak of history and ancient statues lurk in shadowy caves. The north's charm lies in contrasts: clear lakes mirroring mountains and intricate shrines resting in deep forested groves vie for attention with peaceful towns known for mastering a single craft, colourful parks famed for their flower gardens, specialist foodie towns and lesser-known bamboo glades. At the heart of it all are Nikko's temple complexes, where gold leaf glows beneath ornate wood carvings and cedars older than the shoguns themselves. It's a region governed by the seasons. In spring, wisteria tunnels bloom; in autumn, ginkgo streets flame yellow; in winter, snow-hushed landscapes turn villages into postcards.

LAKE CHUZENJI, P 78

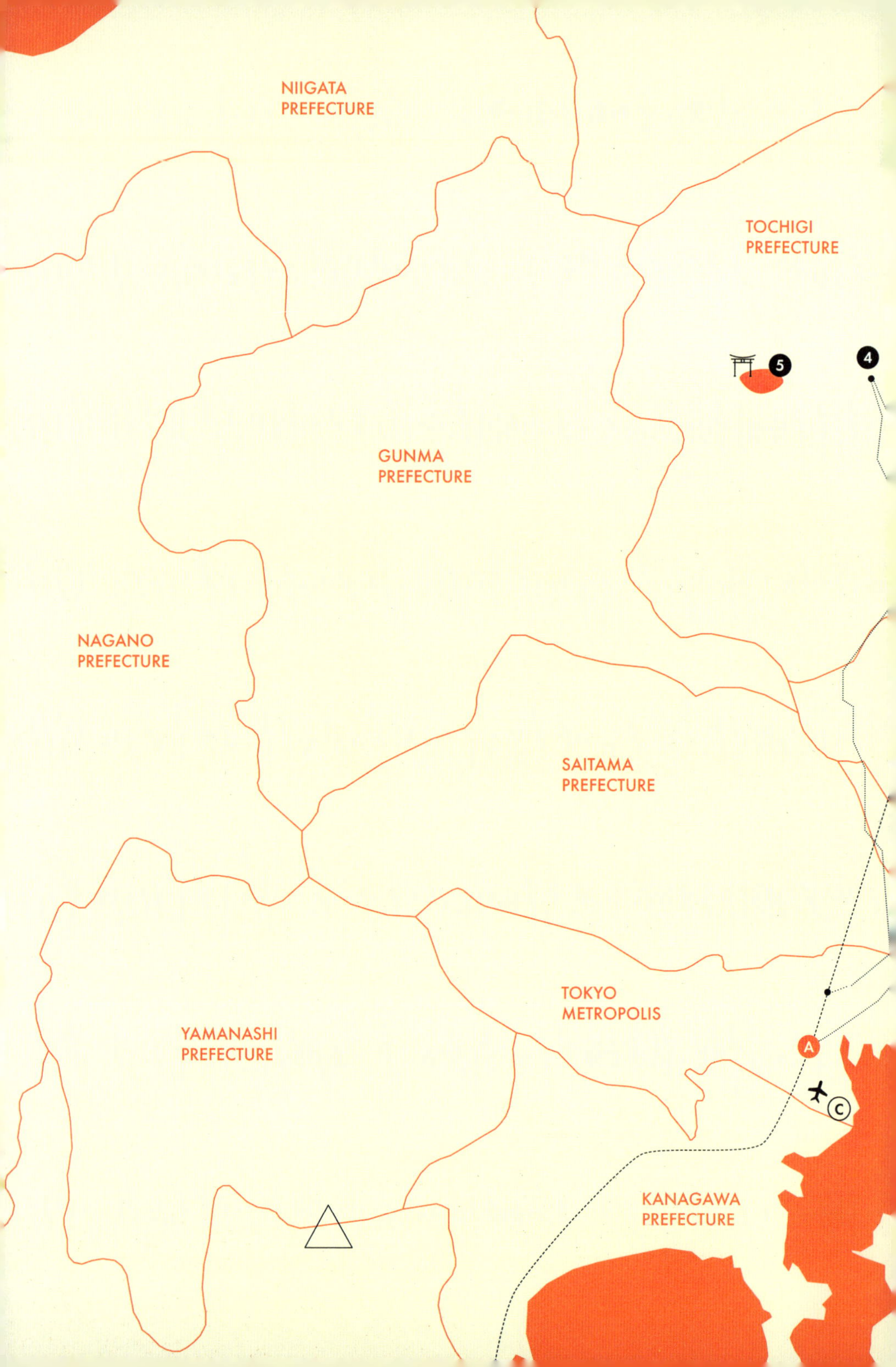

NIIGATA PREFECTURE
TOCHIGI PREFECTURE
5
4
GUNMA PREFECTURE
NAGANO PREFECTURE
SAITAMA PREFECTURE
TOKYO METROPOLIS
A
YAMANASHI PREFECTURE
C
KANAGAWA PREFECTURE

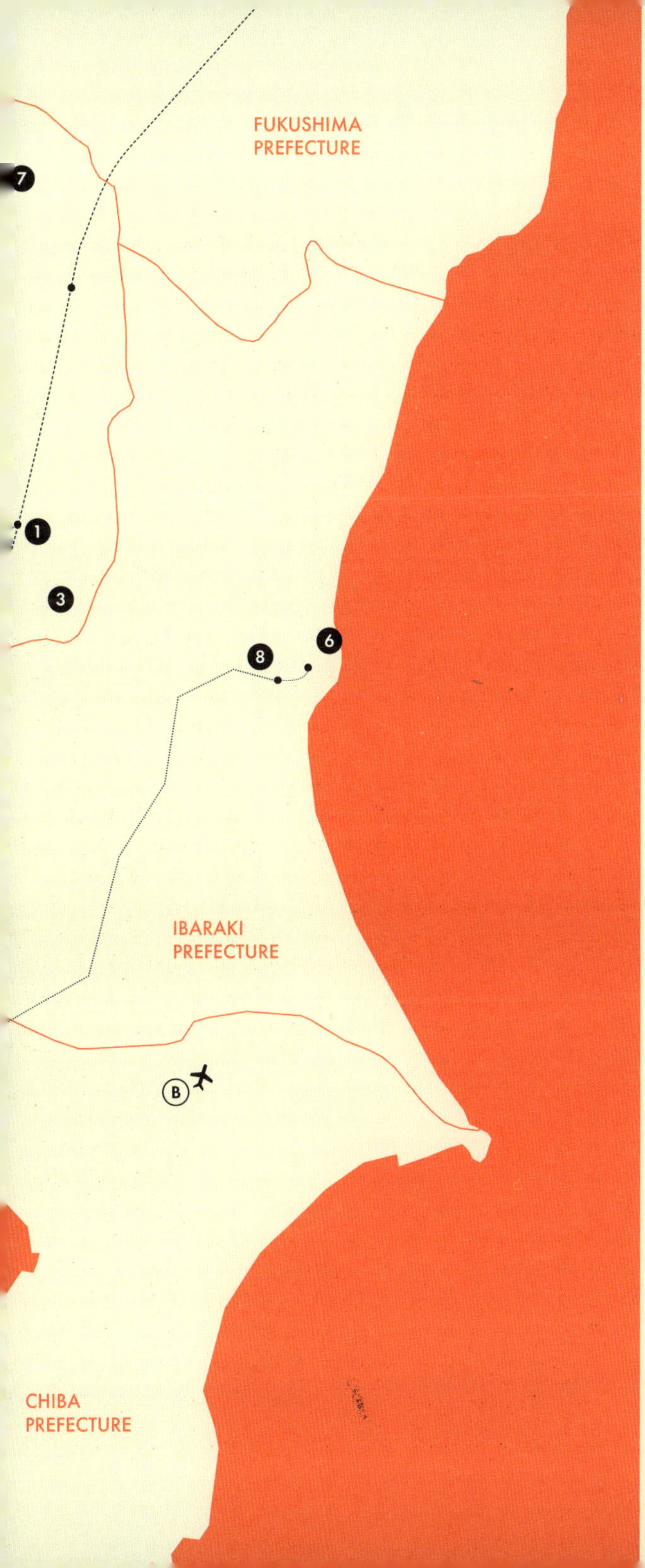

NORTH DAY TRIPS

1. Gyoza in Utsunomiya
2. Sacred Sites in Utsunomiya
3. Pottery in Mashiko
4. Historic Nikko
5. Nikko's Lake Chuzenji
6. Hitachi Seaside Park
7. Shika-No-Yu Onsen
8. Kairaku-en Garden

KEY

- (A) Tokyo
- (B) Narita Airport
- (C) Haneda Airport
- Shinkansen Routes
- Local Train Routes
- Mount Fuji

Overnighter & Weekender Ideas

→ Utsunomiya & Mashiko

→ Nikko, Lake Chuzenji & Senjogahara Marshlands Day Walk

GYOZA IN UTSUNOMIYA

Japan's famous town for dumpling lovers

48 min
OR
1 hr 38 min

GETTING THERE

From Tokyo Station, take the Tohoku Shinkansen (48 min), or from Shinjuku Station, take the Shonan Shinjuku Line to Utsunomiya Station (1 hr 38 min). Take the west exit.

city.utsunomiya.lg.jp

DISCOVER

Gyoza, gyoza, Venus of Gyoza statue, more gyoza!

SEASONAL HIGHLIGHTS

All seasons are good for gyoza.

Advice → *Drink beer or sake with your gyoza.*

Overnighter → *Stay overnight and combine this day trip with Sacred sites in Utsunomiya* *(see page 70).*

Gyoza are a classic Japanese 'fast food' – a small dumpling, usually filled with minced pork, vegetables and ginger, fried on the bottom and then steamed so you get the best of both textures, crispy and tender. Like ramen, it's an absolute staple for workers and commuters: quick to cook and quick to eat. Gyoza are perfect as a side dish or as a main meal with other side dishes. They pair beautifully with beer, and while the classic style is ubiquitous, there are many unique and delicious variations.

Utsunomiya is well known across Japan for its gyoza. The city actually has the highest yearly consumption rate of the dumplings per household, and gyoza eateries can be found both in and around the train station, including the popular and easily accessible **Bariron** and **Kouran**. Walking along **Babadori** from Utsunomiya Station to Utsunomiya Tobu Station you'll find a plethora of gyoza eateries clustered in side streets and lanes, especially on **Miyajimachi**, officially nicknamed 'Gyoza Street' in 2018. If you're a true gyoza fan, consider staying for a weekend rather than just a day to get the most out of the many dumpling restaurants (see page 70 for more on what you can do in Utsunomiya). **Gyoza Kai** is recommended for its variety of different styles and shapes (don't forget to take home some of their famous sauce). **Masashi Miyajima** and **Minmin** are also recommended options.

You can't fault the city's dedication to gyoza – you'll even find a famous statue, the **Venus of Gyoza** (Venus wrapped in a gyoza skin), proudly standing outside Utsunomiya Station – along with gyoza lampposts, gyoza manhole covers and the Utsunomiya Gyoza-kai, a gyoza association that holds a gyoza festival every November. Yum!

SACRED SITES IN UTSUNOMIYA

A town famous for gyoza has some surprising landmarks

48 min

OR

1 hr 38 min

GETTING THERE

From Tokyo Station, take the Tohoku Shinkansen (48 min), or from Shinjuku Station, take the Shonan Shinjuku Line to Utsunomiya Station (1 hr 38 min). Take the west exit.

city.utsunomiya.lg.jp

DISCOVER

Oya History Museum, Ooyaji (Oya Temple), Wakayama Bamboo Farm, Heiwa Kannon (Peace Kannon Statue).

SEASONAL HIGHLIGHTS

Spring and autumn: bamboo, red pine, azaleas and lily of the valley.

Weekender → *As well as staying overnight to eat all the gyoza, extend this trip into a weekend away by catching the JR Kanto bus from Utsunomiya Station to nearby pottery town Mashiko (65 min; see page 74) or the JR Nikko Line train to the famous mountain shrine town of Nikko (42 min; see page 76). You can use Utsunomiya as a base and do all three day trips as a mini-break.*

It's not all about dumplings in **Utsunomiya**. The Venus of Gyoza (see page 69) is made from the famed Oya stone, a soft, volcanic rock that is easy to carve. You can discover more about Oya stone at the **Oya History Museum**, about 25 minutes from Utsunomiya Station via bus. There was once a vast quarry here that mined the stone, and now the cavernous spaces have been turned into a spectacular gallery that looks like a monolithic palace built by an alien civilisation. Anyone keen on geology will find the themed exhibitions fascinating, while lovers of contemporary art will marvel at the works perfectly arranged throughout the huge rooms.

From the museum, walk 8 minutes to the 1200-year-old **Ooyaji (Oya Temple)**, a Buddhist temple carved out of the volcanic rock cliff face. Inside is an extraordinary sight: ten Buddha statues are carved into the rock, including the 1000-armed, 4-metre-high (13-foot-high) **Senju Kannon**, carved in the Heian period (794–1185) and regarded as one of Japan's oldest stone statues of the Buddha. Not far from the temple you'll find the **Heiwa Kannon (Peace Kannon Statue)**, a lofty 27-metre (89-foot) war memorial that's carved into a quarry stone face. Completed in 1954, the striking work has stone steps that you can climb for views of the surrounding parklands.

Anyone who has marvelled at Arashiyama's Sagano Bamboo Grove but felt swamped by snap-happy tourists and influencers is in for a real treat in Utsunomiya. Around 30 minutes by train or bus from Utsunomiya Station you'll find the **Wakayama Bamboo Farm**, Japan's largest bamboo farm, where this grass has been cultivated for 350 years by members of the Wakayama family. Bamboo, chestnuts and blueberries are still farmed here, and visitors can enjoy a spot of sublime bamboo forest bathing on the expansive grounds. There are also bamboo-themed craft classes and night-time illuminations. The farm is around 3 kilometres (2 miles) from the Oya History Museum, which is about a 5-minute walk from Oya Temple and the Peace Kannon Statue, so you can easily see all three in a day. If you have time, also visit the **Utsunomiya Museum of Art**, the spectacular **Kanehon Quarry**, **Tagesan Temple** and, if in season, the **Koshi Zakura**, a weeping cherry tree more than 400 years old.

平 和 観

POTTERY IN MASHIKO

A peaceful town with a deep history of ceramics

Shinkansen 48 min

Bus ~1 hr

GETTING THERE

From Tokyo Station, take the Tohoku Shinkansen to Utsunomiya Station (48 min). Take the east exit and transfer to the Kanto bus for Mashiko (~1 hr). The pottery district is walking distance from the Mashiko Bus Terminal.

mashiko-kankou.org

DISCOVER

Pottery festivals in Golden Week (late April to early May) and early November, Mashiko Sankokan Museum of Shoji Hamada, Higeta Indigo Dyeing Studio, pottery classes, studio kilns, Mashiko Tonoike Sake Brewery.

SEASONAL HIGHLIGHTS

Spring: first pottery festival and strawberry harvest. Autumn: second pottery festival, crisp air, kiln fires glowing at dusk.

Overnighter → *We recommend staying overnight if visiting during the pottery festivals – early hours let you browse before the crowds arrive.*

Mashiko is gentle and wistful, a town that hums softly with the rhythm of spinning wheels, kiln fires and slow hands. For more than 150 years, Mashiko has been the heart of folk pottery in Japan, with a philosophy that treasures beauty in simplicity and imperfection, reflected in the narrow streets, winding roads, open fields and rich forests. The spirit of Shoji Hamada, the potter who brought Mashiko to international renown and helped found the Mingei (folk craft) movement, is a palpable presence here. His thatched-roof house and kiln at the **Mashiko Sankokan Museum** are sanctuaries, odes to the vibrant creativity of a simple handmade life. Clay bowls, indigo fabrics, wooden spoons and mid-century furniture are all arranged in thoughtful order, as if he might return at any moment. His kiln feels like it is simply sleeping, waiting for the master's hands to again work the clay. A small gallery of his works and their inspirations shows the depths of his knowledge and the playfulness of his designs.

Rows of rustic shops line **Jyonaizaka Street**, shelves gleaming with glazes of ash green, milk white and deep iron brown. Each bowl speaks of gentle fingers, creative minds and connections between flesh and earth. In spring and autumn, during the **Mashiko pottery festivals**, the whole street becomes a living market – more than 500 stalls set up across fields and lanes, the scents of kiln smoke and festival food mingling in the air. Exploring the pottery studios and magnificent kilns of Mashiko is a highlight. Classes can be found at **Tsukamoto Ceramics**, which holds pottery workshops, and **Mashiko Tougei Club**, which offers a more intense three-day experience in a centuries-old traditional Japanes house.

Nearby, the **Higeta Indigo Dyeing Studio** offers an interesting artistic parallel to the shaping of clay. Inside, vats of indigo swirl and bubble like witches' cauldrons. Classes allow the novice to dye cloth, staining their hands the colour of twilight.

If time permits, visit the **Mashiko Tonoike Sake Brewery**, which has a 100-year history and offers tours and tastings. Made with the same groundwater that softens the clay for pottery, the must-try sake is served in Mashikoyaki sake cups.

At sunset in Mashiko, smoke curls lazily from chimneys, and the light turns the copper of glazed clay. Even the silence feels pliable – hand-thrown with care, moulded by time, the soul of the city forged by the enduring warmth of human hands.

HISTORIC NIKKO

Famed region with abundant nature and a spectacular shrine

1 hr 50 min

GETTING THERE

From Asakusa Station, take the Tobu Spacia or Spacia X to Tobu-Nikko Station (1 hr 50 min). Take the main exit.

visitnikko.jp

DISCOVER

Toshogu Shrine, Shinkyo Bridge.

SEASONAL HIGHLIGHTS

Spring: blossoms. Summer: cool mountain breezes. Autumn: crimson foliage. Winter: frozen waterfalls.

Advice → *If you arrive in Nikko via Tobu-Nikko Station, make sure you visit Nikko Station just around the corner, one of Japan's hidden gems. Dating back to 1890, the station features wonderful period details and upstairs you'll find the preserved first-class waiting room, called the White Room.*

Weekender → *Consider expanding this day trip into a weekend away, by combining it with Lake Chuzenji (see page 78) and the Senjogahara Marshlands Day Walk (see page 82).*

In **Nikko**, the mountains are dressed in cloaks of deep green and peppered with memorable shrines, waterfalls, trees, bridges, lakes and waterways. There is a saying, 'Never say kekko [wonderful] until you have seen Nikko', and you'll understand why when you experience the depth and scope of this place – and it's just a breezy day trip from the capital.

Your experience will begin on the train journey to Nikko, watching skyscrapers and densely packed towns melt away, replaced by rural scenes, fields, rice paddies, rivers and then deep, dark forests. Walk from Tobu-Nikko Station up a road lined by long-standing shops and eateries and framed by not-so-distant mountains, and you'll soon come across **Shinkyo Bridge**, a vermillion arch that spans the tumbling rapids of the **Daiya River**. The word 'picturesque' was invented for just such a scene.

From here, a steep ascent will bring you to Japan's most celebrated mausoleum, the stunning **Toshogu Shrine**. The shrine grounds are extensive and accented by colourful structures in wood and lacquer. Dragons coil around thick beams, gilded blossoms grow over pillars, and the famed 'see no evil, hear no evil, speak no evil' monkey trio can be found perched impudently on a lintel. This was the tomb of Tokugawa Ieyasu, the shogun who unified Japan, a posthumous declaration of strength, beauty and eternity on proud display. He's not buried here; his actual remains rest in Kunozan Toshogu in Shizuoka (see page 99). However, the Toshogu Shrine is a UNESCO World Heritage site, an ornate masterpiece with Shinto and Buddhist elements in a stunning mountain forest setting.

The **Yomeimon Gate**, often called the Gate of the Sun, richly adorned with gold leaf, intricate wood carvings and hundreds of mythical figures, animals and sages, is an early clue to the treasures that lie within. You'll likely love the **Nemuri-neko (Sleeping Cat)** carving, symbolising peace, which can be found near the entrance to Ieyasu's mausoleum. In the elaborate **Honjido Hall** a crying dragon frolics on the ceiling. Continue on a forested path of stone steps that lead to what was once Ieyasu's actual tomb, a solemn memorial surrounded by towering cedar trees.

When we visited, we opted to stay over, drawing the early morning mountain air deep into our lungs and exploring Lake Chuzenji (see page 78) – you might choose to do the same. The area really needs two days to explore, at least. Returning to Tokyo, we found that Nikko lingered in our spirit, sacred and sublime.

NIKKO'S LAKE CHUZENJI

A vast lake surrounded by nature, temples and history

1 hr 50 min

40–50 min

GETTING THERE

From Asakusa Station, take the Tobu Spacia or Spacia X to Tobu-Nikko Station (1 hr 50 min). Take the main exit, then catch a bus to Chuzenji Onsen Stop (40–50 min).

visitnikko.jp

DISCOVER

Lake Chuzenji, Mount Nantai views, Futarasan Chuzenji Shrine, Kegon Falls, the Italian and British embassy summer villas, Mount Hangetsu Observation Deck, lakeside walking trails and the Senjogahara Marshlands Day Walk (see page 82).

SEASONAL HIGHLIGHTS

Spring and autumn: striking foliage. Summer: cool breezes.

Advice → *Try yuba (dried tofu skin) soba, trout dishes and peach juice from local orchards.*

Weekender → *Consider expanding this day trip into a weekend away, combining it with Historic Nikko (see page 76) and the Senjogahara Marshlands Day Walk (see page 82).*

Although perfectly doable as a day trip in its own right, a visit to **Lake Chuzenji** is a perfect overnight extension to your Nikko trip (see page 76) if you have the time – at night the crowds of Nikko thin out and the air becomes even sweeter.

Catch the bus to Chuzenji Onsen Stop, en route to the lake, and experience the 30 hairpin turns of **Irohazaka Road** as they bend dizzyingly past cedar, rowan and maple trees, vivid yellow ginkgo and vibrant azaleas. If you suffer from travel sickness, take your tablets, because you'll want to enjoy the stunning views that reveal themselves as you climb into the clouds. It's worth noting that more than once you might feel like the bus could get too cocky on a curve and topple over the edge. As the twists and turns give way to longer, flatter roads you'll see a vast body of water come into view: sparkling Lake Chuzenji. This lake was born of fire. Some 20,000 years ago, **Mount Nantai** erupted, spilling lava that dammed a river and formed this pristine jewel. The volcano is now a wonderfully symmetrical mountain whose reflection ripples in the lake's crystal surface.

On arrival it's an 8-minute walk to spectacular **Kegon Falls**. The torrent plunges 97 metres (318 feet) before dissolving into a misty spray. In autumn, the cliffs are ablaze with colour, while in winter the cascade freezes into a frozen fall of shimmering blue ice. From Kegon Falls head to **Funenoeki Chuzenji** (boat passenger) Terminal for a hop-on hop-off day cruise that does a 55-minute loop of the lake (closed December to mid-April). You'll find layers of history scattered like driftwood along the shore. Get off at Tachiki Kannon Pier for **Chuzenji Temple**, which dates back to 784 CE. Here you'll find the 6-metre-tall (20-foot-tall) **Tachiki Kannon**, a wooden carving said to be the oldest in the Nikko region. It's carved from a tree that is still rooted in the ground. The upper walkways of the temple have delightful views of the lake. Other treasures include an inner chamber embellished with paintings of more than 100 flower species found around the lake.

Next stop is **Embassy Villa Memorial Pier**, on the shores of the lake, where you'll discover unexpected echoes of Europe. In the late 19th century, foreign envoys fled Tokyo's heat for this cool alpine shore – their villas feel like living history, atmospheric pieces of architecture and time portals to another world. In mid-century style, the **Italian Consulate Villa** surprises with its airy verandahs, where Mussolini's diplomats once sipped espresso while gazing at Mount Nantai. The **British Embassy Villa**, built in 1896, is now a museum filled with photographs, travel trunks and memorabilia. Take tea in the small cafe and enjoy the quiet nostalgia.

There's a timeless rhythm to life around the lake. Wooden boats sway at the docks, ready to take visitors across the water. Fishermen sit patiently, lines waiting for trout and wakasagi, and waves lap against the shore as mountain and sky blend into the lake's shifting surface. Head up to **Mount Hangetsu Observation Deck** to see an impressive view of the volcanic god mountain and its lake – a highland mirror where fire and lava once met the water, and where spirit and nature now gently rest.

Return to the pier and catch the boat to **Shobugahama Pier**. There are several places nearby where you can stay overnight if you like (book ahead). The next day head up through the **Fish and Forest Observation Garden** towards the **Ryuzu Falls** (Dragon's Head Falls) and the beginning of the **Senjogahara Marshlands** Day Walk (see page 82).

Nikko's Senjogahara Marshlands Day Walk

You can choose to do this hike and Lake Chuzenji (see page 78) as part of a long day trip or overnight stay. If you'd like to do the hike, explore the lake and visit Nikko's Toshogu Shrine, it's best to stay for two nights. For this hike, bring layers – the highland air can be brisk, even in summer.

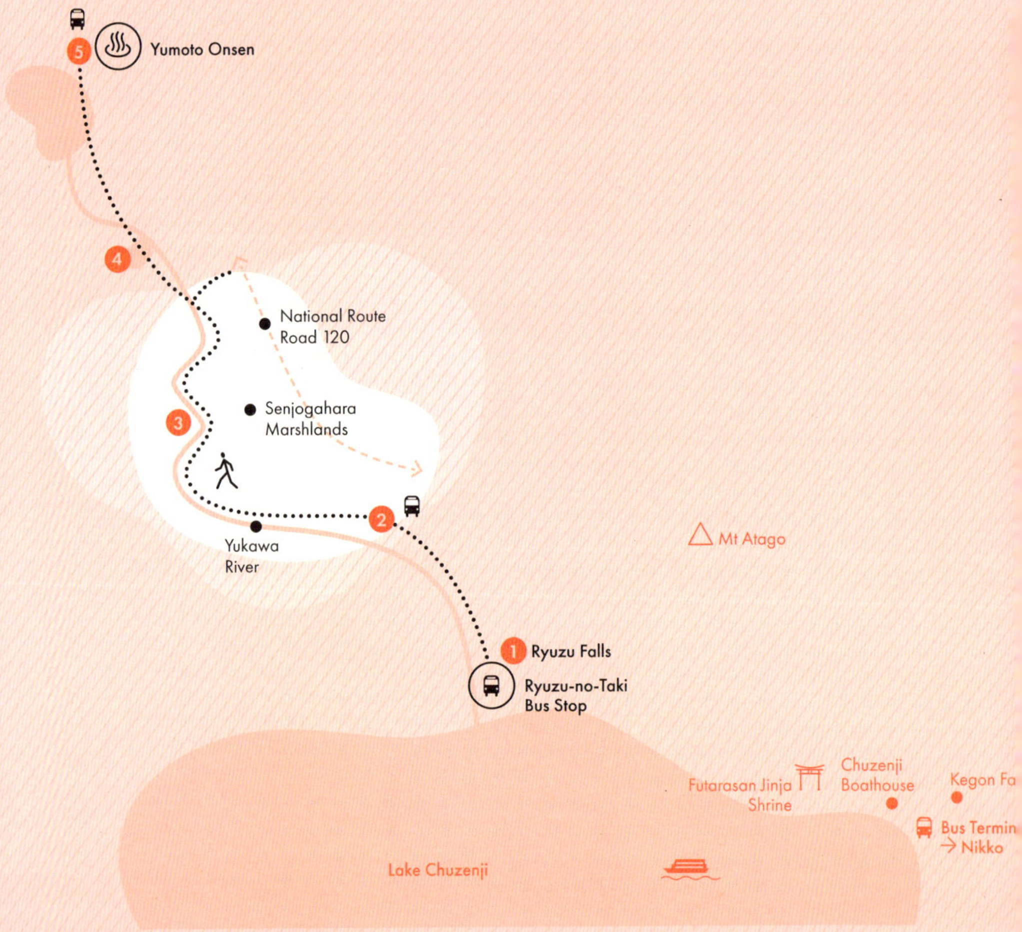

Distance: ~6 kilometres (~3.7 miles) | Duration: 2.5–3 hours | Difficulty: Easy to moderate

1 START AT RYUZU FALLS

Begin your hike from the Ryuzu-no-Taki Bus Stop. Before setting off, admire the twin cascades of Ryuzu Falls, one of Nikko's most iconic sights. The name comes from the way the water splits around a large rock, resembling a dragon's face. Spectacular in autumn, this dragon-head waterfall is framed by trees that blaze brightly in October, earlier than many autumn hotspots. This area marks the start of the Senjogahara Marshlands, a high moorland at about 1400 metres (4593 feet) above sea level.

2 ENTER THE SENJOGAHARA TRAIL

From the Akanuma rest stop area, follow the well-maintained boardwalk that winds through the marshlands. Senjogahara means Battlefield Plain, named for a legendary clash between the mountain gods of Nantai and Akagi in ancient mythology. As you walk, the landscape opens into sweeping golden marsh grass spread out before distant peaks – most notably Mount Nantai, which stands sentinel over the horizon.

3 STOP AT ONE OF THE OBSERVATION DECKS FOR BIRDWATCHING

The wooden observation platforms offer panoramic views and the opportunity to spot wildlife. The marsh is home to Siberian stonechats and wagtails. In summer, cotton grass and alpine blooms colour the fields.

4 CONTINUE TOWARDS IZUMIYADO POND

The trail meanders through light larch forests and open fields, offering glimpses of Izumiyado Pond. In autumn, fiery reds and golds wash the landscape, while in winter, the boardwalk is often cloaked in snow, creating an atmosphere of quiet serenity.

5 FINISH AT YUMOTO ONSEN

End your hike at Yumoto Onsen and reward yourself with a relaxing bath at one of the onsen hotels or Onsen-ji Temple. Alternatively, revive tired feet at the town's free foot bath (check opening times as both the temple and foot bath can be closed in winter). It's also a wonderful place to stay the night.

Take a local bus to return to Lake Chuzenji.

HITACHI SEASIDE PARK

A living canvas of flowers, sky and sea

~90 min (train)

15–20 min (bus)

GETTING THERE

From Ueno Station, take the JR Joban Line Limited Express to Katsuta Station (~90 min). Take the east exit, then catch a local bus to Hitachi Seaside Park (15–20 min).

hitachikaihin.jp

DISCOVER

Miharashi Hill, flower gardens, cycling paths, open lawns, coastal atmosphere.

SEASONAL HIGHLIGHTS

Spring: nemophila blue fields (especially late April to early May). Summer: sunflowers, zinnias, seaside picnics. Autumn: red kochia and cosmos blooms (October). Winter: quiet walks, wide skies, coastal stillness.

Advice → *The bus from Katsuta Station arrives at the west entrance and bikes can be hired from just inside the gate.*

Hitachi Seaside Park and Kairaku-en Garden (see page 89) can be combined into one day trip.

We love Ibaraki Prefecture, a places of sea breezes, endless horizons and vast stretches of land adorned with flowers, fields and folklore. **Hitachi Seaside Park** harnesses the region's mystical ability to grow flowers. They don't simply bloom here; they transform the landscape itself. Entire hills are painted with colour, living strokes on a canvas of green.

Hitachi Seaside Park is sizeable. As well as its flower gardens, it offers several walking trails, restaurants, picnic areas and a small amusement park. A train trundles on tyres through the park, stopping at various locations to allow visitors to get on and off at will. Rental bikes are a great way to explore the park's many cycling paths. Hire one from just inside the west gate and cycle past the narcissus garden, towards the old-style Japanese house **Miharashi no Sato** and the charming **Omoyo Old Village**.

The beauty of the flowers, mass planted in large fields in the park, cannot be fully captured in words or photographs; you have to experience it, so go in your favourite season if you can. Spring dresses the park in blue. The nemophila fields roll across **Miharashi Hill**, millions of delicate blossoms opening in the gentle air. Walking among them feels dreamlike; the earth and sky blend into a single palette of azure, set against the glinting sea. In autumn, red kochias cast off their summer coats of feathery green and cover the hills with orbs of crimson fire. From the top of Miharashi Hill, the red waves spill down to the sea, spectacular against the silver-blue horizon. Cosmos flowers add splashes of pink and white.

Summer brightens the park with greens and yellows. Sunflowers turn their happy faces towards the sun, and zinnias ripple in the fields, while you can rest in shaded groves with a picnic, the shadows and the ocean breeze offering cool relief. In winter, the park sleeps, grasses dry, the sea winds sharpen, the flowers lie silent. Hitachi Seaside Park is a landscape as fleeting as it is eternal – flowers bloom and fade, and each visit is different, each season a renewal.

SHIKA-NO-YU ONSEN

A thousand years of healing at a rustic onsen with very hot water

~75 min

50 min

GETTING THERE

From Tokyo Station, take the JR Tohoku Shinkansen to Nasushiobara Station (~75 min). Take the main exit, then catch a local bus to Nasu Yumoto Onsen village (50 min) and walk to the bathhouse (2 min).

shikanoyu.jp

DISCOVER

A historic bathhouse, the unique kaburi-yu ritual, surrounding Nasu Highlands and volcanic landscape.

SEASONAL HIGHLIGHTS

Autumn: crisp air, autumn foliage around the bathhouse. Winter: early morning steam, mineral-rich water in warming baths.

Advice → *Showering with soap is not permitted inside the bathhouse – this is a therapeutic onsen. Be prepared for a very high water temperature and bring a towel and a full water bottle. Go on weekdays or in the early morning hours for a quieter experience.*

In the Nasu Highlands, where mist floats like ghosts between pine trunks and volcanic memory stirs the earth, **Shika-no-Yu** spans a ravine – an onsen born of legend and shaped by time. The hot spring was reportedly discovered more than 1300 years ago when a wounded deer was found healing in its waters. The onsen's name means deer hot spring, and the healing powers of these ancient, mystical waters are still available to the adventurous bather.

The air might feel cold from the early morning when you arrive and cross the threshold of the wooden bathhouse. Built in 1941, the rustic wooden exterior is simple and inviting. A white sign bearing the cute illustrative logo shaped from kanji hangs stark against the dark wood. Bamboo blinds provide modesty over the bath windows. Inside, the water is milky pale, mineral-rich and sulphurous, flowing through six pools of ascending heat – between 41 °C and 48 °C (106–118 °F) – each softly labelled, a gentle warning.

Before entering, join the ritual of kaburi-yu – pouring the hot water over your head about 200 times both for the body's circulation and for courage. The water is regarded as good for a list of ailments: neuralgia, fatigue, skin malaise and high blood pressure among them. It promises relaxation and release. You'll find the scent of sulphur strong, cedar boards warm and worn underfoot.

When we visited, we emerged with flushed skin tingling. We spoke of our experience – did we venture past the second or third bath? No. Bathers had been sitting, chatting, wrapped in towels, just next to the top bath, the hottest. Had they ventured in? Were they veterans?

Outside, snow-capped peaks rise in the distance, the Nasu volcanoes watching approvingly while you soak. Afterwards, wander into the forest of birches nearby, the tall trees conversing above in hushed rustling whispers, the highland air cool.

Shika-no-Yu is a pilgrimage and a promise, water and memory. Healing and history. The deer that was once healed here now roams only in legend – but the undoubting spirit of recovery and renewal remains.

KAIRAKU-EN GARDEN

A beautiful plum blossom grove in one of Japan's top three gardens

~80 min

15 min

OR

30–40 min

GETTING THERE

From Ueno Station, take the JR Joban Line Limited Express to Mito Station (~80 min). Take the north exit. Kairaku-en Garden is a short bus ride (15 min) or a 30–40 minute walk away. Buses depart regularly during plum blossom season.

ibaraki-Kairaku-en.jp

DISCOVER

Plum Blossom Forest, Kobuntei Pavilion, Tokugawa Museum, Senba Lake, the bamboo grove and cedar forest.

SEASONAL HIGHLIGHTS

Spring: plum blossoms (early March), azaleas and wisteria (April–May). Autumn: colourful foliage.

Advice → *Visit early morning to see mist rising over Senba Lake and plum petals drifting like snow; combine the trip with the nearby Kodokan School, once a school for teaching the ways of the samurai to the local samurais' children.*

Hitachi Seaside Park and Kairaku-en Garden (see page 89) can be combined into one day trip.

Kairaku-en Garden, one of the Three Great Gardens of Japan, is like a living scroll, the beating heart of Mito, a garden built not just for beauty, but for shared joy. Established in 1842 by Tokugawa Nariaki, the ninth lord of Mito, it was named 'a garden for everyone's pleasure'. Given that gardens at the time were strictly for the enjoyment of the nobility, this was a radical gesture.

Today, that spirit is still alive in every path and petal. The garden's most memorable moment comes in early spring, when 3000 plum trees burst into pink, white and crimson clouds. Their fragrance is strong in the cool air – sharp, clean and an emphatic promise that winter has finally turned. Locals stroll in yukata (casual cotton kimono), vendors pour sweet ume-shu, and the sound of laughter flits among the trees like birdsong. The vibrantly coloured rows of plum blossom rival their more famous cousin, the cherry blossom, or sakura.

At the centre of the luminous display you'll find the **Kobuntei Pavilion**, once a literary retreat for the lord himself. Its wooden floors creak softly beneath your feet; from its upper verandah, look down upon the plum forest and across to **Senba Lake**, where drifting swans ripple the silver surface. Not far from here, you'll find shaded paths lined with towering bamboo and ancient cedars with magnificent gnarled roots.

Kairaku-en Garden is wondrous at any time; each season reshapes the garden – spring's blazing azaleas, autumn's golden leaves, winter's stillness. Yet the blessings of nature's grace are felt most keenly during plum blossom time.

For us – wandering along the cedar path, petals clinging to our shoes, the evening slowly descending like a curtain going down on a spectacular day – we felt once again that in Japan's strolling gardens there is a kind of mystical energy that settles within, a joy that can be called upon whenever peace, tranquillity and beauty are needed.

SOUTH

South of Tokyo, the land exhales into salt air, sunlight and the long sway of the Pacific Ocean. This is coastal Japan at its most nostalgic: fishermen mending nets on quiet wharves, seafood markets clattering awake at dawn, and beaches where families have played for generations. Shrines perch on cliffs glazed with sea spray; islands float like jade beads across Sagami Bay; and old pilgrimage routes wind through temple forests scented with pine and incense. The south is where Tokyo escapes to breathe – to surf, to soak in seaside onsen, to eat flame-grilled kinmedai (golden-eye snapper) or sashimi fresh enough to bring tears. In summer, the coastline glitters; in winter, the skies sharpen, revealing Mount Fuji rising pure and luminous across the bay. Villages cling to hillsides, lighthouses sweep the sea, and ferries drift between islands like slow-moving prayers. Southward day trips carry the balm of the ocean: restorative, windswept and profoundly freeing.

IZUKYU-SHIMODA, P 112

NAGANO
PREFECTURE
SAITAMA
PREFECTURE
YAMANASHI
PREFECTURE
KANAGAWA
PREFECTURE
SHIZUOKA
PREFECTURE
12
11
13
10
9
8
4
1
3
2
5
6
1
1
7

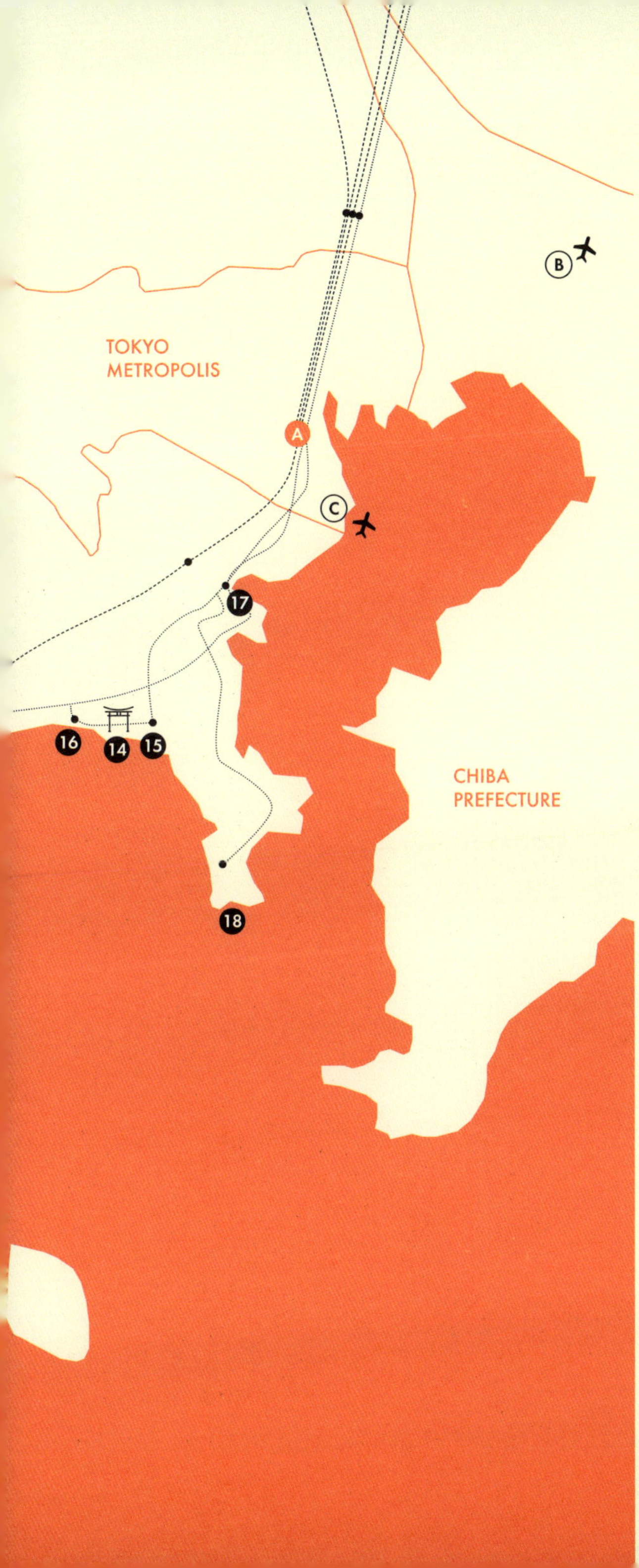

SOUTH DAY TRIPS

1. Tea in Shizuoka
2. Nihondaira Yume Terrace
3. Miho No Matsubara
4. Mishima
5. Shuzenji Onsen
6. Mount Omuro
7. Izukyu-Shimoda
8. The Sea & Steam of Atami
9. MOA Museum of Art
10. Odawara Art Foundation Enoura Observatory
11. Volcanic Hakone
12. Art in Gora
13. The Old Tokaido Road
14. Zen Kamakura
15. Vintage Kamakura
16. A Seaside Sojourn in Enoshima
17. Noodles in Yokohama
18. Miura & Jogashima Island

KEY

- A Tokyo
- B Narita Airport
- C Haneda Airport
- •---• Shinkansen Routes
- •·····• Local Train Routes
- △ Mount Fuji

Overnighter & Weekender Ideas

→ Shizuoka, Nihondaira Yume Terrace & Miho No Matsubara

→ Atami, MOA Museum of Art & Odawara Art Foundation Enoura Observatory

→ Hakone, Gora & The Old Tokaido Road

TEA IN SHIZUOKA

A tea museum and tea plantations with views of Mount Fuji

~1 hr

35 min

23 min

GETTING THERE

From Tokyo Station, take the Tokaido Shinkansen to Shizuoka Station (~1 hr). Take exit I, A or E. For Kanaya, take the JR Tokaido Local Line to Kanaya Station (35 min). For Kakegawa, from Kanaya Station, take the Tokaido Local Line to Kakegawa Station (23 min).

exploreshizuoka.jp

DISCOVER

Shizuoka Tea Museum, terraced tea fields stretching before Mount Fuji, Shizuoka tea shops and the cobbles of Kanaya-zaka on the Old Tokaido Road.

SEASONAL HIGHLIGHTS

Spring: first tea harvest, cherry blossoms. Summer: lush greenery, chilled tea, forest walks. Autumn: terraces, warming tea, striking views. Winter: crisp air, steaming cups beside frost-touched gardens, Mount Fuji.

Advice → *Kakegawa Station is a Shinkansen station – it takes 1 hr 40 minutes to reach Tokyo directly.*

Weekender → *Expand this day trip into a weekend away by combining it with Shizuoka Nihondaira Yume Terrace (see page 98) and Miho no Matsubara (see page 102).*

Set in the soft foothills of Mount Fuji, **Shizuoka** is one of the country's most revered tea-growing regions, where entire valleys seem tuned to the rhythm of cultivation. At Shizuoka Station you'll smell the tea instantly: a deep, earthy perfume that mingles with cedar resin and the honeyed scent of wildflowers.

Kanaya is a quiet town that is home to the **Shizuoka Tea Museum** (a 5-minute bus or taxi ride from Kanaya Station), a must-visit for anyone curious about the culture that shaped these hills. Here, you can trace tea's journey from ancient China to modern Japan, explore exhibits of rare tools and handcrafted teaware, and taste region-specific brews in a serene tearoom overlooking a delightful strolling garden where Mount Fuji peeks over the garden wall. Matcha is brewed low and slow, its aroma rising in delicate ribbons of steam. The museum also offers workshops – blending sessions, roasting experiences and casual tastings that will leave you with a deeper understanding of why this region's tea is so loved. Around the museum, tea fields spread out in billowy rows and you can wander the tiny paths threading between the hedges. Fuji overlooks the fields, creating a wonderful opportunity for you to take photos of the mountain impressively guarding the precious tea. Before returning to Kanaya Station, explore **Kanaya-zaka**, a stretch of the **Old Tokaido Road** that is girded by rich forest and paved with cobblestones. Take sturdy shoes as the cobbles are hard to walk on.

Head to **Kakegawa** and visit **Ninomaru Tea House** on the grounds of **Kakegawa Castle**. The castle towers over the city, high on a hill. Dating from the 1400s, and in ruins for many years, it was renovated in 1994 using traditional methods. The tea house, a sukiya-style traditional building, has tatami rooms serving tea and wagashi, presented like small, edible jewels. It is a premium tea experience, with views over a perfect Japanese garden or onto the towering turrets of the castle. You can even rent the space for private tea ceremonies if you want tea with friends.

Shizuoka has a gentle pace, pulling your gaze outward towards the mountain but always bringing you back to the warmth of a teacup held in your hand. If you have time after your perfect tea day, or if you're staying over, make sure you visit Shizuoka city's tea shops. At **Maruzen Tea Roasters**, cups of single-origin sencha and gyokuro are brewed to perfection, their flavours delicate. Don't miss the picture-worthy kakigori, where you get three types of matcha to pour over your iced treat. Other tea shops of note are **Nanaya Shizuoka**, **Kinzaburo**, **Chato Matcha and Bakery**, **Chagama** and **Aardvark Tea Astand**.

NIHONDAIRA YUME TERRACE

Views of Fuji and the bay from an architectural walkway above a mountain shrine

~1 hr

30 min

GETTING THERE

From Tokyo Station, take the Tokaido Shinkansen to Shizuoka Station (~1 hr). Take the Keyaki-dori exit. Local buses connect to Nihondaira Yume Terrace (30 min).

nihondaira-yume-terrace.jp

DISCOVER

Nihondaira Yume Terrace, the Nihondaira Ropeway, Kunozan Tosho-gu Shrine.

SEASONAL HIGHLIGHTS

Spring: clear skies, blossoms near Nihondaira Yume Terrace. Summer: sea breezes, strawberries. Autumn: crisp air, vivid sunsets over Fuji. Winter: snow-capped Fuji vistas.

Advice → *Catching a bus from Shizuoka Station to Nihondaira Yume Terrace and buying a return ticket for the ropeway is likely your best option for a day trip. Start early as Mount Fuji is often shrouded in clouds from late morning onwards.*

Weekender → *Expand this day trip into a weekend away by combining it with Tea in Shizuoka (see page 94) and Miho no Matsubara (see page 102).*

Shizuoka unfurls between mountains and sea, a place where cedar and salt mingle and Mount Fuji hovers like a guardian spirit. As you wander this region, you'll realise how layered it is: ancient trade routes, Tokugawa history, fishing villages, tea fields, shrines and one of Japan's most poetic coastlines. Kengo Kuma's spectacular **Nihondaira Yume Terrace**, an observation deck made from local timber, floats high on the mountain and takes in that majestic coast. The deck gives you a memorable panorama: the Shimizu Port stretching out towards Suruga Bay, the blue immensity of the Pacific Ocean and, of course, Mount Fuji, lording over it all. A clear day is your best friend, and as the song says, 'you'll feel like you can see forever'.

The nearby **Nihondaira Ropeway**, an aerial lift that opened in 1957, also has sweeping views of the area, particularly spectacular in autumn, when the mountain foliage is ablaze. You can see all this on the way down to **Kunozan Tosho-gu Shrine**, the *actual* resting place of Tokugawa Ieyasu (see page 77), established in 1617. Note the striking red buildings in the Gongen-zukuri style, especially the **Romon Gate** and the **Drum Tower**. The shrine grounds are quite extensive and various buildings are adorned with ornate and colourful carvings. You'll find Ieyasu's mausoleum at the top of the shrine steps. If you have the energy, you can also get to the shrine by climbing up more than a thousand stone steps from the coast. Ganbatte! (Do your best!) It's easier to go down, of course, and although the ropeway ticket includes a return journey, the walk down the steps leads to the coast, home to one of Japan's premier strawberry regions. If you do this, don't miss out on a fresh strawberry juice or a soft-serve ice cream. The stores will happily call you a taxi, and Miho no Matsubara (see page 102) is not far away.

We visited Miho and Nihondaira Yume Terrace on the same day, going easy on ourselves by catching a few taxis. Another good option is to make it an overnight or weekend stay: explore Nihondaira Yume Terrace before heading to Shizuoka city's tea shops (see page 94), then stay over in Shizuoka city to visit Miho no Matsubara the next day. You can also add Kanaya (see page 95) to create a perfect matcha-meets-Fuji itinerary.

MIHO NO MATSUBARA

Mount Fuji vistas from a pine forest and beaches of black sand

~1 hr

40 min

GETTING THERE

From Tokyo, take the Tokaido Shinkansen to Shizuoka Station (~1 hr). Take the south exit. Local buses connect to Miho no Matsubara (40 min).

miho-no-matsubara.jp

DISCOVER

Miho no Matsubara Beach, pine forests, iconic Fuji views, black sand coast.

SEASONAL HIGHLIGHTS

Spring: clear skies. Summer: sea breezes. Autumn: crisp air, vivid sunsets over Fuji. Winter: snow-capped Fuji vistas.

Advice → *If you feel like a ride across the bay, catch a local train from Shizuoka Station to Shimizu Station, then a free shuttle bus to Shimizu Port. Catch the ferry to Miho Marina, just west of Miho no Matsubara Beach.*

Bikes and e-bike hire are available at Shimizu Port, S Pulse Dream Plaza and other locations.

Weekender → *Expand this day trip into a weekend away by combining it with Tea in Shizuoka* *(see page 94)* *and Nihondaira Yume Terrace* *(see page 98)**.*

There are many memorable Fuji views in Shizuoka, but one combines several elements to show the mountain in a unique light. From Shizuoka Station, catch a bus to the edge of **Miho no Matsubara**. Suddenly, the world expands.

Before you stretches a forest of more than 30,000 ancient black pines, many hundreds of years old, planted during and protected since the Heian period. Their trunks rise in sculptural twists; their needles whisper in long, wind-drawn sighs. As you step beneath their canopy, you'll feel as though you've entered an older Japan – one shaped by myth. Stroll the **Miho no Kami-no-Michi**, the God's Road, a straight, sacred path leading to **Miho Shrine**, where the celestial maiden Hagoromo's legend still lingers in incense and silence.

Pass through a small patch of the forest, which opens towards the sea, and there it is: Mount Fuji rising immense and radiant, watching over black volcanic sand and wind-ruffled pines. The mountain appears almost suspended – a perfect triangle, its flanks smudged by drifting cloud. With the waves curling white against the black sand, nature's palette feels deeply elemental: pine green, sea blue, earth charcoal, Fuji's peak dusted with snow.

Follow the coast on the paved cycling road, a beautiful 7-kilometre (4-mile) curved walk around the peninsula. At its far tip lies **Miho no Matsubara Beach**, where driftwood gathers like sculptures and Fuji shifts from dusky lavender to diamond white as the sun climbs. This is the same place that once inspired renowned artists Hiroshige and Hokusai, whose woodblock prints made this very view immortal in paintings such as *Pine Grove of Suruga Bay* and *Thirty-six Views of Mount Fuji* respectively.

If you're visiting in summer, stop to buy local tomatoes from vending machines by the roadside – ruby red, sun warmed, impossibly sweet – the perfect final flavour of a day shaped by sea light, mountain breath and the pine-scented poetry of Shizuoka.

MISHIMA

A city shaped by its waterways and watched over by Mount Fuji

45–60 min

OR

~2 hr

GETTING THERE

From Tokyo Station, take the Tokaido Shinkansen to Mishima Station (45–60 min). Take the north exit. Local Tokaido Line trains also connect Tokyo and Mishima (~2 hr).

mishima-tourism.jp

DISCOVER

Mishima Skywalk, Mishima Taisha Shrine, Genbe River strolling path, Rakujuen Garden.

SEASONAL HIGHLIGHTS

Spring: cherry blossoms at Mishima Taisha and gardens. Summer: cool stream walks, river festivals, skywalk views. Autumn: foliage in Rakujuen Garden. Winter: clear skies for the most vivid Fuji views.

Advice → *Mishima is known for unagi (eel) raised in pure spring waters, then grilled over charcoal and lacquered with sweet soy. Also try the Mishima croquette, made from the local Bareisho potato.*

Downstream of the snows of Mount Fuji, **Mishima**'s streets burble with underground rivers feeding pure springs, flowing into ponds, streaming through canals and coursing softly beneath bridges and gently arched willows. Just north of Mishima Station, the springs converge in the **Genbe River**, a glinting band of water where carp flit beneath the surface and ducks float on it. Large stepping stones form a path in the river where you can wander peacefully while locals wade the river's shallows and children scoop water with bamboo dippers. In season, festivals light the river with lanterns that drift on the current like fireflies. Visit the nearby **Rakujuen Garden**, once housing a daimyo's, or lord's, villa, and stroll its paths featuring thick green moss, large stone lanterns, quiet ponds and impressive pine trees.

A couple of minutes from Rakujuen, and part of a history walk of the area, you'll find **Mishima Taisha**, a shrine where vermillion bridges span lakes, impressive camphor trees tower above and zelkova wood pavilions impress with their intricate carvings. Sacred deer, brought in from Nara, roam the grounds (you can feed the deer; food can be purchased at the shrine). At dusk, large stone lanterns flicker into light. Samurai once prayed here before campaigns, and poets wandered seeking fortune; today, couples pass beneath the sacred trees for blessings. On clear days, Fuji appears, casting its blessings over the shrine. In spring, the shrine's cherry blossoms are impressive bursts of pale pink, reflected in ponds fed by Fuji's meltwater. In August, you'll be able to watch the **Mishima oh Matsuri**, the Mishima Grand Festival, with its excited crowds, thunder of drums and parade of detailed and colourful floats carried from the shrine to Mishima Hirokoji Station.

From Mishima Station, catch the Tokai bus for 20 minutes to the **Mishima Skywalk**, which stretches 400 metres, or a quarter of a mile, across a vast valley. The longest pedestrian suspension bridge in Japan, it's one of Mishima's major drawcards, as, on clear days, grandiose Mount Fuji rises majestically before you, the emerald depths of Suruga Bay glittering far below. The morning is a good time to go and the clearest days are usually in November.

SHUZENJI ONSEN

Picturesque walks, hot springs and a history of tea in a strollable town

45–60 min

35 min

10 min

GETTING THERE

From Tokyo Station, take the Tokaido Shinkansen to Mishima Station (45–60 min), then transfer to the Izuhakone Railway Sunzu Line to Shuzenji Station (35 min). Take the main exit for buses and taxis to Shuzenji Onsen (10 min)

izunokuni-tourism.com

DISCOVER

Shuzenji Temple, Bamboo Grove Path, Katsura River, Hie Shrine, Shuzenji Nijino Sato, Mount Daruma Observatory.

SEASONAL HIGHLIGHTS

Spring: sakura (cherry blossom) along the Katsura River. Summer: iced matcha, mossy shade, cool river air. Autumn: colourful maple leaves. Winter: steam rising from open-air baths.

Advice → *Wear walking boots and carry an onsen kit. Onsen bathing is available at the town's public bath, Hakoyu, and some ryokan have day bathing. Buy local bamboo craft and stop for a beer made from Shuzenji's pure waters at Baird Brewery Gardens (enjoy it with a view of the Kano River).*

South of Shizuoka and Mishima, **Shuzenji Onsen** can be found in a strollable onsen town where tea, steam and time exist in harmony. The **Katsura River** runs through the heart of the town, a constant gentle burble. Over its network of stone bridges hang paper lanterns and willow branches, and along its edge stand tatami-lined tea houses, sliding doors open to gardens of moss, ponds and sculptural stone. Cups of sencha are poured with patience and enjoyed while reflecting on the streams and forested glades. Here, one of the treats is soft-serve ice cream with the freshest wasabi from the famous nearby farm. Try it: it works.

In Shuzenji's onsen, the body steeps in hot mineral water as tea leaves do in a cup. The two acts mirror each other: immersion, warmth and the quiet unfolding of something deeply relaxing. Explore the area and you'll find the **Bamboo Grove Path**, its lofty green towers arched, swaying with the rhythm of the wind. Peeking between the stalks are small cafes, serving roasted hojicha, smoky and warm, alongside wagashi that tastes of the seasons – pale-pink sakura-shaped sweets in spring, chestnut buns in autumn and cooling, slightly bitter and slightly sweet matcha ice cream in summer. At the **Shuzenji Temple**, founded in 807 CE by the monk Kobo Daishi, monks still teach zazen meditation to those who seek to calm the mind as gently as the body (Tuesdays, 9.30 am). In autumn, the surrounding leaves blaze brilliantly against the spectacular temple backdrop. Near the temple you can also see the atmospheric **Shigetsuden**, the Izu region's oldest wooden structure, which has a golden statue of a merciful Buddha inside.

As the light begins to fade on your day, follow the path west to **Mount Daruma Observatory** for another great Mount Fuji view – the mountain gazes down as if in quiet approval of the healing onsen waters.

In Shuzenji, time doesn't pass; it brews. Each season pours its moods into the valley – tea, mist, maple, snow – and when you leave, you'll carry that warmth inside.

MOUNT OMURO

Ride the cable car up to the top of a dormant volcano with astounding views

~50 min

OR

2 hr 39 min

~45 min

+

20 min

GETTING THERE

From Tokyo Station, take the Tokaido Shinkansen to Atami Station (~50 min). Or, from Tokyo Station take the Odoriko Line to Atami Station (2 hr 39 min). Transfer to the Izu Kyuko Line to Izu-Kogen Station (~45 min). Take the main exit. From there, a 20-minute bus or taxi ride will take you to the Mount Omuro Lift Station.

omuroyama.com

DISCOVER

Mount Omuro, chairlift, summit loop trail, Mount Fuji views, Yamayaki Festival.

SEASONAL HIGHLIGHTS

Spring: newly green grasses, clear Fuji views. Autumn: brilliant sunsets. Winter: golden grasses, annual Yamayaki Festival (mid-February).

Advice → *Make a stop on the way back at Ito Station to visit splendid Tokaikan, a former ryokan built in 1928, which has a spectacular frontage. If you're an onsen enthusiast, time your trip to include a visit to Akazawa Hot Springs Pavilion (with impressive views), only 15 minutes on a free shuttle bus from Izu-Kogen Station.*

Mount Omuro is a smooth, symmetrical volcano with a perfect bowl-shaped caldera that gently rises up from the Izu landscape. Omuro is more of a presence than a mountain – serene, mystical and curious. Its sides are covered in grass that shifts from emerald in spring to burnished gold in summer and burnt black in winter, making Omuro a living canvas for the seasons and the shifting light.

Take the chairlift that ascends slowly, nearly skimming the slope. At the summit, follow the trail that circles the rim in a breezy 1-kilometre (0.6-mile) loop, a perfect contemplative walk where the crater, now sleeping, hums with the memory of fire. Torii gates and Buddha statues add a sacred element to the mountain while food vendors and souvenir stalls give it a festive air.

The crater confidently faces off with some spectacular views: the Pacific sparkling to the east, Mount Fuji rising in the distance, the thin white line of the surf curling against the Izu Peninsula. Each step around the crater brings a new view – a vast open sky, shadows across grass, mountainous terrain, Petit Hotel's glamping pods, the Ito Country Club golf course.

We visited on a clear day and can safely say that the Fuji view from Omuro's peak is one of our all-time favourites. There's something about being that high up and that close, bringing you almost level with the sacred mountain, that is truly spectacular.

In mid-February, fire makes a symbolic return to the volcano. During the **Yamayaki (mountain burning) Festival**, the mountain is literally set ablaze, its dry winter grass flaring into orange light against the deep blue of the sky – a burning-off ritual of renewal that has been practised for centuries. By spring, new green shoots emerge, and soon, once again, Omuro is verdant, replenished and vibrant. Standing alone with the wind, sky and grass, you feel the surprising satisfaction that the symmetrical beauty of a parabolic curve can bring. Standing atop Omuro at sunset is to stand inside a haiku – poetic, majestic, infinite.

おおむろ軽食堂
大室山 登山 リフト 乗車口
Mt.OMURO LIFT
おおむろふもと売店

IZUKYU-SHIMODA

A bay of black ships and the temple where Japan opened to the world

~2 hr 40 min

OR

~50 min

1 hr 40 min

GETTING THERE

From Tokyo Station, take the Limited Express Odoriko Line to Izukyu-Shimoda Station (~2 hr 40 min). Take the main exit. Or from Tokyo Station, take the Tokaido Shinkansen to Atami Station (~50 min), then transfer to the scenic Izukyu Line to Izukyu-Shimoda Station (~1 hr 40 min) – ride the Kurofune Black Ship–themed train if you can.

izukyu.co.jp

DISCOVER

Ryosen-ji Temple, Perry Road, Shimoda Black Ship Museum, Shirahama and Tatadohama beaches, Mount Nesugata Ropeway, Shimoda Park hydrangeas.

SEASONAL HIGHLIGHTS

Spring: camellias and hydrangeas, ideal walking weather. Summer: turquoise seas, surfing, swimming, fireworks over the bay. Autumn: clear skies, quiet beaches. Winter: mild coastal days, perfect for onsen and coastal hikes.

Advice → *Bring sunscreen, shoes for uneven stone paths and small bills for cafes. If you want to swim, check beach flags and signs for swimming conditions (Pacific surf can be rough).*

At the far southern curve of the Izu Peninsula, **Shimoda** meets the ocean with a kind of weathered elegance – part seafaring port, part dreamy beach town, part open-air history book. As the train drifts along the coastline, large windows framing cliffs and white-tipped waves, you'll feel yourself leaving Tokyo's pace behind and slipping into a slower, saltier rhythm.

Shimoda is where Japan's closed gates first swung open. In 1854, Commodore Matthew Perry's *Kurofune* – the infamous steam-powered Black Ships – dropped anchor in this quiet bay, their dark hulls reflected in waters that had known only fishing skiffs and trading boats. That encounter, bristling with politics and possibility, reshaped the nation. It's integral to the lore of the town: the black ship appears on manhole covers, in museum exhibits, as sightseeing cruises that mimic the gunboats themselves and even in the charming Black Ship–themed train that delivers you here, with its mini-gallery displaying wildlife, maritime lore and the dramatic meeting of worlds.

Walk to **Ryosen-ji Temple**, where in 1855 the Treaty of Peace and Amity was signed, nudging open the door to international exchange. The temple is still hushed, still ringed with camphor trees, their magnificent gnarled trunks showing age and wisdom. Standing in its gravel courtyard, you might feel that crossroads in history – the weight of decisions that rippled outwards across oceans.

But Shimoda is not only history. **Shirahama Beach**'s white sands curve in perfect arcs; **Tatadohama Beach** thrums with surfers riding glass-green waves. The Pacific crashes against volcanic rock, flinging salt spray into the wind. The palms sway lazily.

Spend time on **Perry Road** – a canal-side street lined with old kura warehouses and willows whose branches dip into the water. Stone bridges arch over drifting koi. Antique shops spill over with lacquered boxes, sea-weathered maps and glass bottles that perhaps once floated across oceans carrying messages.

Night drapes Shimoda in a quiet, silken veil. The waves murmur stories of merchants, samurai and travellers long gone. This town is not merely a destination. It is a reminder of endurance; of openness; of the delicate balance between past and present; the meeting of land, sea and history; and the junction of what once was, and what has now become.

温泉まんじゅう
阿部商店
温泉まんじゅう
いらっしゃいま

Retro resort chic, fresh seafood and seaside ambience

~50 min

OR

1 hr 40 min

GETTING THERE

From Tokyo Station, take the Tokaido Shinkansen to Atami Station (~50 min). Or from Tokyo Station, take the local JR Tokaido Line to Atami Station (1 hr 40 min). Take the main exit.

city.atami.lg.jp

DISCOVER

Hashiriyu, onsen ryokan with ocean views, seaside seafood markets, beachfront and fireworks festivals.

SEASONAL HIGHLIGHTS

Spring: cherry blossoms in Atami gardens. Summer and winter: fireworks festivals.

Advice → *Kiunkaku, a former villa, mixes Japanese tatami rooms with stained glass and Art Deco flourishes. The former ryokan was built in 1919 and features a preserved, tiled room designed as a Roman bath.*

Weekender → *Expand this day trip into a weekend away by combining it with MOA Museum of Art (see page 116) and Odawara Art Foundation Enoura Observatory (see page 118).*

Atami has long been the coastal town where Tokyoites escape the city for relaxation – so long, in fact, that it now exudes a nostalgic, faded glamour by the sea, giving the place a desirable time-travelling ambience. The name itself means hot ocean, and that is the essence – water in every form, steaming, sparkling, endlessly shifting. And with that water come beachside vistas, sea bathing and, most of all, onsen, where you can soak away your cares, often with a stunning view of sparkling **Sagami Bay**.

Atami is never shy about spruiking its pleasures. Along **Heiwa-dori Shopping Street**, you can wander through a corridor of colour and nostalgia: vendors calling out welcomes, steam rising from trays of onsen manju (sweet buns puffed soft in hot spring vapour), and the air thick with the scent of roasting seaweed and freshly caught fish. Here, kinmedai – the prized golden-eye snapper of the Izu seas – hang on racks to dry, their salted skins catching the breeze. Beside them, stalls overflow with spiny lobsters, dried squid and citrus piled like golden treasure.

The street gives the sense of a time tunnel: a living fragment of the Showa era, where neon signs flicker above retro arcades, plastic food displays glow warmly behind glass and old cafes still serve cream sodas in delicate fluted glasses.

The shoreline of Atami curves in a crescent, fishing boats bob on the waves and palm trees line the streets. The town is almost a mini-Riviera. At night, the sea glitters with squid boats, their lamps rising and falling like fireflies on the horizon. Climbing into the hills, forested slopes are dotted with ryokan and rotenburo (outdoor baths). Research well so you can book that perfect onsen ryokan, making sure to get a room with one of those stunning ocean views. To explore the region's hot springs credentials further, don't miss **Hashiriyu**, considered one of the three oldest hot spring sources in Japan, at an impressive 1300 years old. Take your time to marvel at the spring, which, unusually, flows horizontally.

Atami is unabashedly both retro and renewed, a place where onsen steam mingles with laughter, where sea air and the scent of grilling seafood fill the lungs. It's a town suspended between eras, glowing with the warm patina of nostalgia yet pulsing with new energy – a shoreline refuge where time loosens its grip and worries dissolve like mist.

MOA MUSEUM OF ART

Architecture, sea and sky meet in a luminous museum

45 min
OR
1 hr 40 min
+
10 min

GETTING THERE
From Tokyo Station, take the Tokaido Shinkansen to Atami Station (45 min). Or from Tokyo Station, take the local JR Tokaido Line to Atami Station (1 hr 40 min). From the main exit, it's a 10-minute bus or taxi ride to MOA Museum of Art.

moaart.or.jp

DISCOVER
MOA Museum of Art, Golden Tea Room, seasonal plum and maple gardens, the Crystal House.

SEASONAL HIGHLIGHTS
Spring: plum blossoms. Summer: clear ocean views. Autumn: bright maples.

Advice → *If you wish to delve more into the Church of World Messianity (the original source of much of the museum's collection), its headquarters, Zuiunkyo, can be found on a hill in Atami. The Suishoden, or Crystal House, is a semicircular building with a glass frontage providing 180-degree uninterrupted views of the ocean.*

Weekender → *Expand this day trip into a weekend away by combining it with Atami* *(see page 114)* *and Odawara Art Foundation Enoura Observatory* *(see page 118)**.*

Atami is not only hot springs and seaside splendour; it is perfectly placed to showcase art in an impressive, natural setting.

Set high on a hillside, the **MOA Museum of Art** frames the ocean as if it were a work of art on display. The approach to the gallery is both seriously immersive and surprisingly contemporary. You'll ride long escalators, climbing through several mirrored, mood-lit tunnels, pausing at the ever-changing patterns of the world's largest kaleidoscope projected onto a colourful ceiling. Stop at the designated photo points to take pictures amid the swirling psychedelic shapes. Head outside for a more sedate scene, with a large courtyard offering an incredible view of the ocean over the shoulders of Henry Moore's *King and Queen*. From here, follow the steps to the gallery, a brutalist concrete bunker built in 1982 as a third space to hold the vast collection of Mokichi Okada, founder of the Church of World Messianity. Inside are painted scrolls, calligraphy, lacquerware, costumes and tea bowls. Also among the gallery's designated National Treasures is Ogata Korin's *Red and White Plum Blossoms* – a vibrant screen painting that pulses with an incandescent spirituality. A spectacular re-creation of 16th-century samurai and feudal lord Toyotomi Hideyoshi's **Golden Tea Room** is adorned with gold leaf and ornate designs, exhibiting his flamboyance and opulence.

The grounds of MOA Museum of Art are as artful as the treasures housed within: stone lanterns, moss-brushed paths and seasonal gardens. In spring, plum blossoms flutter like pale-pink lanterns; in autumn, maples glow red and yellow.

On the museum grounds, **Sobanobou** offers one of Atami's quietest pleasures: handmade buckwheat noodles served in a minimalist wooden dining room that looks out onto sculpted gardens. After lunch, wander to **Ippaku-an**, a tea hut so small and serene it feels like a whispered secret. Here, tea is served the old way: slowly, thoughtfully.

This is the magic of Atami's MOA: it hangs between mountain and ocean like a jewel on a cliff, its architecture framing nature as reverently as scrolls and folding screens. Its art is not confined to rooms of lacquer and gold; it spills outward into gardens, dining rooms and teahouses and into the infinity of the sea.

ODAWARA ART FOUNDATION ENOURA OBSERVATORY

A multidisciplinary contemporary art space that overlooks Sagami Bay

90 min
OR
45 min
7 min
+
5 min

GETTING THERE
From Tokyo Station, take the Tokaido Ueno Tokyo Line to Nebukawa Station (90 min). Or from Tokyo Station, take the Tokaido Shinkansen to Odawara Station (45 min), then take the Tokaido Line to Nebukawa Station (7 min). There is a free shuttle bus from Nebukawa Station to Odawara Art Foundation Enoura Observatory (5 min) (bookings essential).

odawara-af.com/en/enoura

DISCOVER
The Optical Glass Stage, the Summer Solstice Light-Worship 100 Meter Gallery, the Winter Solstice Light-Worship Tunnel.

SEASONAL HIGHLIGHTS
Seasonal shifts in light and landscape, citrus groves in bloom and fruit. Special sunrise viewings are held on the solstices and equinoxes.

Advice → *Tickets for events held on the solstices and equinoxes are by advance lottery reservation only.*

Weekender → *Expand this day trip into a weekend away by combining it with Atami (see page 114) and MOA Museum of Art (see page 116).*

We'd seen pictures of **Odawara Art Foundation Enoura Observatory** before we visited – hewn stone walkways reaching out towards the ocean, a platform of glinting glass absorbing the sunrise, sparse buildings made from natural materials hidden in groves of hinoki cypress and tangerine. But pictures will never do it justice. This is not a place to display art. It's a conduit for the magical properties of stone, wood, light and time.

Famed contemporary artist, Hiroshi Sugimoto established the Odawara Art Foundation in 2009, and Enoura Observatory opened in 2017 both as the headquarters of his foundation and as his poetic ode to art, the sea and the land – all of which come together in a sculpture garden that uses its surrounds to spectacular effect.

Weather-beaten wood, the fallen bodies of ancient trees, and rocks made jagged by time are interspersed with contemporary sculpture – works carved or constructed both onto and into the land, seemingly existing beyond it. The **Optical Glass Stage** sits before an amphitheatre as if waiting for nature to rise from the sea and the forest to perform a play. As the sun reflects off the ocean, so it shimmers on the surface of the stage, and both the stage and the sea beyond seem in harmony. Next to the stage you'll find one of the observatory's standout works, a cantilevered rusted red metal corridor that tapers into a ledge from where you can view the beauty of the ocean while seemingly floating above it.

Nearby, the **Summer Solstice Light-Worship 100 Meter Gallery** has the same effect, jutting out towards the infinite blue. Its spiritual sibling, the **Winter Solstice Light-Worship Tunnel and Light Well** is hit by divine light as the sun rises or descends in the sky.

Don't miss **Uchoten Teahouse**, with its stone torii gate, sitting in a grove as if it has always been there.

Entry is strictly by reservation only (you'll be allotted a visiting time). Limited numbers are allowed in for each reservation, so you'll never feel overwhelmed or rushed here. If you're expecting a typical museum with walls and label art, Enoura Observatory isn't that. It's something beyond – a reminder to stop, observe and absorb. It's spiritual, gentle and sublime, light-years from our fast-paced, tech-driven contemporary world.

VOLCANIC HAKONE

Hot springs, steaming mountains and spectacular Fuji

~90 min

OR

35 min

15 min

GETTING THERE

From Shinjuku Station, take the Odakyu Romancecar to Hakone-Yumoto Station (~90 min). Or from Tokyo Station, catch the Tokaido Shinkansen to Odawara Station (35 min), then transfer to the Tozan Railway to Hakone-Yumoto Station (15 min). Take the main exit.

hakone-japan.com

DISCOVER

Lake Ashi and Hakone Shrine's red torii gate; Hakone Tozan Railway; Hakone Shrine and Tenzan; Kayoi Toji Ikkyu and Yunosato-Okada onsens.

SEASONAL HIGHLIGHTS

Spring: cherry blossoms by Lake Ashi. Summer: hydrangeas, cool mountain air. Autumn: colourful foliage across valleys. Winter: clearest Fuji views over the lake.

Advice → *Try Hakone's black eggs, boiled in its volcanic waters, which are said to add seven years to your life.*

Weekender → *Combine this day trip with Art in Gora (see page 124) and the Old Tokaido Road (see page 126) if you have a couple of days.*

An easy day trip from Tokyo, **Hakone** is a world of volcanic activity, steaming vents, hot springs and impressive mountains, all presided over by a godlike Mount Fuji. Hakone is a place of many moods: lake mist, sulphur smoke, maple red in autumn, hydrangea blue in June. Coming here is a contract to accept a slower pace of life, one measured in hot spring baths and shifting Fuji views, Tokyo's frenetic pace a distant memory. For centuries, travellers paused here along the Tokaido Road to relax their weary bodies before crossing the mountain passes.

From Hakone-Yumoto Station, the eclectic **Tozan Railway** begins a rattling, groaning and very enjoyable ascent to Gora Station. From here it's a steep ropeway trip to Sounzan Station and then an alarmingly high cable car climbs further up the mountain. Sweeping panoramas of thriving nature, scarred earth, steam and sky are your reward. The Owakudani region is the mountain's breath made visible. The air is thick with minerals, pungent and sulphurous. Pools bubble, milky turquoise and grey. The sound is constant: a low hiss, the restless sighing of a planet denied full release. It feels ancient, like a hum at the dawn of creation.

From a mountain vantage point at Ubako Station, you'll see vast **Lake Ashi** glimmering below. Head down to the lake and catch a boat out to its distant centre to see Mount Fuji rising majestically behind the mountains. The famed red torii of **Hakone Shrine** rises from the water's edge, reflected in the lake, a wonderful photo opportunity from the boat, or head through the forest to the shrine for a popular picture, standing beneath the vermillion gate with the water of Ashi sparkling behind you. Further along you'll find the **Hakone Komagatake Ropeway**, an oft-overlooked cable car that takes you to a peak with staggering views of Mount Fuji and Sagami Bay where you'll find **Mototsumiya Shrine** and its tori gate that frames the shrine on one side and the bay on the other.

The landscape is lush and elemental. As a volcanic town, Hakone has plentiful and memorable hot springs, and after a day of exploring, you'll find that nothing can beat a hot springs bath. Some are in hotels that open up for day bathing, some are in legendary, historic spaces and some are in shiny new complexes. **Yumoto**, **Gora** and **Miyanoshita** individually hold clusters of inns where steaming baths have spectacular mountainside vistas. Recommended day-bathing onsen include atmospheric, old-world **Tenzan**; **Kayoi Toji Ikkyu** for an onsen in forested surrounds; and **Yunosato-Okada**, a contemporary super sento. Enduringly popular, Hakone is filled with delights that rejuvenate, invigorate and inspire.

ART IN GORA

Art and nature in perfect harmony near Hakone

At the heart of Hakone's mountains lies **Gora**, a town where gardens and galleries flourish amid hot springs hotels and vibrant nature. Unlike the dramatic sulphur vents of Owakudani or the open waters of Lake Ashi (see page 121), Gora is about refinement, manicured landscapes, hillside ryokan and, of course, art.

The crown of Gora is the **Pola Museum of Art**, a building designed to become one with the forest. Glass walls in vast spaces allow trees and sky inside while walkways hover over moss and beech. The collection celebrates Impressionism, perfect in such an impressionistic landscape – Monet's lilies, Renoir's colour, Cézanne's soft, angular mountain forms. Japanese painters who reimagined this European sensibility enter the conversation too. From the museum, paths thread into the surrounding woods. In autumn, the canopy of trees burns crimson and gold, framing the museum's lantern-like structure. In spring, wildflowers bloom along the trails.

The town offers moments of cultivated pause. **Hakone Gora Park** blooms with roses in summer, blue hydrangeas in June rain, and maples in October. Its French-style layout feels naturally European, but the backdrop is unmistakably Japanese, giving the garden a unique look and feel.

Back on the Tozan Railway, step off at Chokoku-no-Mori Station, where art finds a natural home. The **Hakone Open-Air Museum** spreads sculptures across lawns and valleys, the works of Henry Moore, Picasso and Japanese masters standing beneath changing skies, as if alive. Children clamber over artful structures created for play and reflection. The pieces seem eternal, celebrating the environment, mimicking the natural forms of the region or standing defiantly before it as a colourful and sometimes humorous contrast. The location is sublime, the air fresh; the monumental mountains embrace the sculptural shapes like long-lost friends.

After a day of Impressionism, light and colour, the hot water of an onsen will feel like another layer of art – transient, shimmering, softening the skin. Hakone is a vibrant tapestry, but in Gora, a refined weave threads the region's stories – art and nature a powerful, resonant theme.

Train	~90 min
Train	40 min
Bus	8 min

GETTING THERE
From Shinjuku Station, take the Odakyu Romancecar to Hakone-Yumoto Station (~90 min), then transfer to the Tozan Railway to Gora Station (40 min). The Pola Museum has a free shuttle bus from Gora Station (8 min).

hakone-japan.com

DISCOVER
Pola Museum of Art (Impressionists, contemporary art and forest setting), Hakone Open-Air Museum, Hakone Gora Park.

SEASONAL HIGHLIGHTS
Spring: flowers in Gora Park. Summer: cool mountain air, hydrangeas. Autumn: foliage around Pola Museum. Winter: snow-dusted silence, museum in silver light.

Advice → *Evenings in Gora belong to the onsen ryokan, where private baths peer out onto delightful hillside views of perfectly manicured gardens.*

Weekender → *Combine this day trip with Volcanic Hakone (see page 120) and the Old Tokaido Road (see page 126) if you have a couple of days.*

THE OLD TOKAIDO ROAD

An historic Hakone trail with towering cedars

———— Train ~35 min

············ Bus ~40 min

GETTING THERE

From Tokyo Station, take the Tokaido Shinkansen to Odawara Station (~35 min), then transfer to the Hakone Tozan bus for Moto-Hakone (~40 min).

Trail start: Moto-Hakone (near Hakone Shrine Torii Gate).

Trail end: Hakone Sekisho Checkpoint or Hatajuku (depending on route).

Distance: ~2.5 kilometres (~1.5 miles) (main cedar-lined section); allow 1.5–2 hours at a leisurely pace.

hakone-japan.com

DISCOVER

Cedar Avenue, Hakone Sekisho Checkpoint, historical markers and a gentle atmosphere.

SEASONAL HIGHLIGHTS

Spring: mist and moss. Autumn: crisp air, amber leaves. Winter: silent forests, fewer visitors.

Advice → *Bring good walking shoes, water and light rain gear.*

Weekender → *Combine this day trip with Art in Gora (see page 124) and Volcanic Hakone (see page 120) if you have a couple of days.*

The Old Tokaido Road once carried samurai, pilgrims and poets between Edo (Tokyo) and Kyoto, their sandals stepping the exact same cobbles that still pave the road. In **Hakone**, the past lingers in moments like these, where you can still place your feet on their path – the same uneven stones, the same hush beneath towering trees.

Begin in **Moto-Hakone**, where **Lake Ashi** laps quietly on its shores. The trail climbs over mossy cobblestones, worn smooth by centuries of footsteps. You'll soon enter **Cedar Avenue**, planted over 400 years ago by the Tokugawa shogunate to shade travellers. It's a living colonnade with majestic trunks, tortured roots snaking across the paths, and canopies through which filtered sunlight dapples the ground.

Halfway along, you'll find ishidatami, small stone guide-markers that are inscribed with inspiring haiku as well as the extensive distances to Edo.

As the path emerges near the **Hakone Sekisho Checkpoint**, where officials once inspected documents and goods, the forest opens to views of Lake Ashi, still and silent, mirroring the sky. The checkpoint was one of the most important security posts on the Tokaido, a reminder that this was a road not just of poetry, but of politics and power.

You may have only walked a few kilometres, but centuries will seem to have passed. It's a moving experience, imbued with history, coloured by mystical light and countless stories and lives. Yet in the end it's all about those cedar trees, sentinels standing watchful, seemingly propping up the sky and the clouds – their shadows stretching long across the stones as if urging us to carry forward the memory of all who passed before. The walk along the Old Tokaido Road is a deep reminder that every journey, no matter how small, becomes part of something vast, enduring and profoundly human.

ZEN KAMAKURA

Zen temples and zazen meditation to rival Kyoto

~55 min

GETTING THERE

From Tokyo Station, take the JR Yokosuka Line to Kita-Kamakura Station (~55 min). Take the main exit.

visit.trip-kamakura.com

DISCOVER

Engaku-ji, Jochi-ji and Kencho-ji Zen temples.

SEASONAL HIGHLIGHTS

Spring: camellias, azaleas. Summer: hydrangeas. Autumn: maples, crisp air. Winter: crisp cedar scent.

Advice → *If you have time, Meigetsu-in Temple (the famed (Hydrangea Temple), with its wonderful circular window, is within easy walking distance of these zen temples. Hokoku-ji is a 35-minute walk from Kencho-ji Temple (also called the Bamboo Temple); it's another Rinzai Zen temple that offers zazen meditation.*

Both Zen and Vintage Kamakura (see page 132) can be done in a day.

Just beyond Tokyo, a constellation of Zen temples offers a depth and stillness that rivals Kyoto's finest. It feels almost improbable to find such sanctuaries this close to the capital, so slip past Kamakura's usual crowds and wander into the world of **Kita-Kamakura** – where towering gates, ancient forests and the rhythm of your breath offer the perfect counterpoint to Tokyo's restless hum.

Catch the train to tiny, charming Kita-Kamakura Station. A short walk will bring you to **Engaku-ji**, one of Kamakura's Five Great Zen Temples, founded in 1282 to honour those who died in the Mongol invasions. Its purpose has always been peace: carved into wood, echoed through stone, expressed in silence.

There's a zazen meditation practice at dawn, when the temple is still shrouded with mist. Inside the Butsuden, the temple's main building, a monk strikes the wooden han; its sharp crack slices the early morning hush, focusing the mind. This zazen at Engaku-ji is free, meeting at 5.50 am and beginning at 6 am. The first JR Yokosuka Line train from Tokyo Station reaches Kita-Kamakura just in time for the session. If you prefer a gentler schedule, Engaku-ji also offers afternoon zazen on Saturdays and the first and third Sundays of the month, from 2.30 pm to 4 pm, for a small fee.

Maples frame the temple's entrance gate, which in turn leads to the towering Somon Gate. Wander to the **White Deer Cave**, the ogane (great bell) and the grave of film director Yasujiro Ozu. Dry gardens and bamboo groves complete the tableau – quiet, composed, deeply Zen.

A short stroll from here takes you to **Jochi-ji**, founded in 1283, intimate and moss-softened. Statues of Buddhist figures Amida, Miroku and Shakyamuni stand like stone sentinels between shaded paths. Ozu once lived here; writer Tatsuhiko Shibusawa rests here. There is no public zazen, but the temple itself feels like a long, unbroken breath – perfect for contemplation.

Walk on for a few minutes to **Kencho-ji**, Japan's oldest Zen training monastery, built in 1253. Its long, ceremonial axis draws you inward: the Sanmon Gate, the Butsuden and the Hatto, where a vast dragon coils across the ceiling. The unique Zen garden ripples with curved patterns like wind on water ready for night-time illuminations. Zazen is held at Kencho-ji on Fridays and Saturdays, 3.30–4.30 pm, for an admission fee; chairs available.

In between meditations, you will roam narrow lanes draped in maples and strewn with lanterns. As the train carries you back towards Tokyo, watch the light fade behind the hills and embrace the quieter version of yourself.

VINTAGE KAMAKURA

Treasure hunting in a treasured land

~1 hr

GETTING THERE

From Tokyo Station, take the JR Yokosuka Line or Shonan Shinjuku Line to Kamakura Station (~1 hr). Take the east exit for Komachi-dori, vintage shops and kissaten (traditional coffee shops), and the west exit for curated vintage boutiques.

visit.trip-kamakura.com

DISCOVER

Kitanoya, Iwata Coffee Shop, Milk Hall, Tsubame Cafe, Tsurugaoka Hachiman-gu Shrine.

SEASONAL HIGHLIGHTS

Spring: cherry blossoms. Summer: beaches and festivals. Autumn: brilliant foliage. Winter: crisp, quiet streets; cafe culture at its cosiest.

Advice → *Explore early to beat crowds; many kissaten have limited seating. Bring cash for smaller vintage shops. Don't forget to pick up some Hato Sabure, dove-shaped butter biscuits, the famous omiyage (souvenir) of Kamakura. You can buy them in Tokyo, but get them here from the beautiful main store.*

Both Vintage and Zen Kamakura (see page 128) can be done in a day.

Temples and sea breezes usually come to mind when thinking of **Kamakura**, but if you're a lover of all things vintage, you'll arrive chasing a different kind of pilgrimage – one stitched in old fabrics and glowing with kissaten nostalgia. Just outside Kamakura Station's east exit, you'll merge with the crowds flowing towards **Komachi-dori**, a street beloved by teens for its croquettes, mochi skewers and taiyaki. Yet amid the sugar rush and selfies, two treasures wait.

Look for a mannequin in kimono, its sleeve drifting slightly in the breeze. Up a narrow staircase lies **Kitanoya**, a tiny vintage trove stacked with kimono, yukata, haori and obi – silks and cottons lined up in rainbows. Sift through drawers of fabric scraps and patterned scarves, the kinds of pieces that once lived entire lives and now speak of new possibilities. Prices are surprisingly gentle; temptation, unavoidable.

A few steps closer to the station, the heavy wooden door of **Iwata Coffee Shop** appears and ushers you back to 1945: chrome trim, leather booths, lace around frosted glass. This kissaten is famous for its pancakes – two thick, golden discs that take 20 minutes to make and are worth every second of the wait. The pancakes are best enjoyed alongside a melon cream soda or a perfect fruit sando.

But Kamakura's kissaten culture unfurls far beyond Komachi-dori. Nearby, **Milk Hall** will pull you in with its whimsical signboard and jazz drifting out the door. Inside, warm lamps glow over shelves of curiosities: wooden toys, odd antiques, postcards curling softly at the edges. Try omurice and the house-blend coffee – both comforting, memorable.

To the west of the station, the vintage scene deepens. **Forest Vintage** and **Chapter Vintage** lean into 1950s Americana and Ivy style, while **re;la valeur** curates high-end labels. **Tsubame** and **Butter Vintage** continue the treasure hunt with garments that speak of earlier eras. As a counterpoint, **Hatsune Antiques** displays Edo-era swords and kimono with reverence.

By late afternoon, head to **Tsubame Cafe** and sip tea while admiring cabinets of Edo and Meiji antiques. Kamakura reveals itself not as a single story, but as countless threads – a tapestry stitched in old fabrics, steeped in kissaten coffee and softened by the fingerprints of decades.

A SEASIDE SOJOURN IN ENOSHIMA

Beachside nostalgia on a curious island

~1 hr

~15 min

~25 min

GETTING THERE

From Tokyo Station, take the JR Tokaido Line to Fujisawa Station (~1 hr), then transfer to the Enoden Electric Railway for Enoshima Station (~15 min). Walk across the Enoshima Benten Bridge to the island (~25 min).

discover-fujisawa.jp

DISCOVER

Enoshima Shrine; Samuel Cocking Garden and Sea Candle; Iwaya Caves; Benzaiten Nakamise Street; Enoshima Rock Coast; and Chigogafuchi.

SEASONAL HIGHLIGHTS

Spring: flowers, Fuji views. Summer: beaches, festivals, sea breezes. Autumn: crisp air, clear panoramas. Winter: best visibility for Fuji.

Overnighter → *Turn this day trip into an overnighter by catching the charming Enoden Electric Railway to Kamakura's Zen temples, with some vintage shopping on the side (see pages 128 and 132).*

The island of **Enoshima** rises from the water like a myth – small enough to cross in an afternoon, yet somehow holding shrines, gardens, sea caves, legends and the entire summer childhood of Tokyo. From Fujisawa Station, take the **Enoden Electric Railway** to the island; you'll feel the shift immediately as the little train rattles along the coast, salt wind rushing through open windows, surfers carving black silhouettes into the foam. And if she's feeling generous, Mount Fuji appears – aloof, luminous, a grey-blue guardian hanging above Sagami Bay.

Hop off at Enoshima Station and follow the road south until the **Enoshima Benten Bridge** appears. The current span dates to 1962, but the link itself – between mainland bustle and island magic – has existed since 1891. As you cross, gulls wheel overhead like impatient guides, and the scents of seaweed, tide and frying snacks rise from the shoreline.

The bridge takes you to **Benzaiten Nakamise Street**, a sloping lane where old-fashioned shops cling to the hillside. Shell charms glint in the sun, grilled octopus crackers snap beneath wooden paddles, and ice creams melt faster than tourists can eat them. The vermillion of **Enoshima Shrine** appears – dedicated to Benzaiten, goddess of music, arts and all things that stir the heart. Legend says she subdued a five-headed dragon here; perhaps his spirit still curls around the island's caves and lanterns.

Climb upwards to the **Samuel Cocking Garden**, founded in 1880 by the British merchant whose name it bears. A curious fusion of Victorian whimsy and coastal Japanese calm, it unfolds with camellias, tropical palms, warm greenhouse air and the slender height of the **Enoshima Sea Candle**, an observation tower and lighthouse. From the lighthouse deck, you'll see Sagami Bay gleaming like spilled silver. To the south lie the hazy folds of the Izu Peninsula; to the west, Fuji rises – if she hasn't tucked herself behind the clouds.

Further on, the island tapers into rock and wind. Here lie the **Iwaya Caves** – two ancient hollows carved by waves and once visited by monks, sailors and the occasional dragon. Candlelight trembles across statues and altars; the stone breathes cool air. A pathway above the sea leads to the **cave of Gozuryu**, the dragon Benzaiten tamed. Here, clap your hands, just as tradition asks, and wait for the dragon to appear.

By dusk, the Sea Candle glows like a lantern of the gods. Couples drift along the dark beach; the waves sigh; the bridge draws you homeward, salt on your sleeves, the island's many stories of holidays, adventure and discovery now part of your own.

NOODLES IN YOKOHAMA

A city's obsession with soba and udon

~25 min

11 min

10 min

~15 min

20 min

GETTING THERE

From Tokyo Station, take the JR Tokaido Line or Keihin-Tohoku Line to Yokohama Station (~25 min), then catch the Blue Line to Shin-Yokohama Station (11 min). Take exit 10 and walk 10 minutes to the Shin-Yokohama Ramen Museum. Back at Shin-Yokohama Station, catch the Blue Line (~15 min) to Sakuragicho Station. Take the North 2 exit and walk 20 minutes to the Cup Noodles Museum.

yokohamajapan.com

DISCOVER

Shin-Yokohama Ramen Museum, Cup Noodles Museum, Sankeien Garden, Yokohama Chinatown, noodle eateries.

SEASONAL HIGHLIGHTS

Spring: sakura (cherry blossom), strolls to ramen stops. Autumn and winter: cool air and hot broth perfection.

Advice → *Yokohama's Sankeien Garden, dating to 1906, is one of Japan's best gardens and features a renowned public swimming pool.*

Yokohama has always been Japan's port of first tastes – where ideas and flavours arrived before the rest of the country even knew their names. It was here, more than a century ago, that ramen came ashore from China and began its long, slow simmer towards becoming Japan's favourite comfort food. Today, for the noodle pilgrim, Yokohama is a secular temple – where broth, steam and nostalgia mingle to create the perfectly chewy atmosphere.

Begin your pilgrimage at the **Shin-Yokohama Ramen Museum**, where a surprisingly detailed replica of a 1958 Tokyo ramen alley bustles beneath low lantern light. Nine different ramen shops line the ersatz streets inside, each from a different prefecture – from Hokkaido's creamy miso to Kyushu's rich tonkotsu. You can order mini-bowls, tasting your way through Japan's geography of broth and losing yourself in a delicious kind of time travel. It's a culinary amusement park that conjures up a surprising authenticity. As an added bonus, ramen workshops provide the opportunity to assemble your own ramen from scratch.

From there, take the Blue Line to Sakuragicho Station; the **Cup Noodles Museum** sits on the waterfront, an impressive square glass-and-steel bento box. Inside, the history of instant ramen unfolds with whimsical reverence: Momofuku Ando's invention retold through colourful exhibits and walls lined with decades of cup designs, from the retro to the contemporary. Upstairs, a cup noodle can be crafted by choosing noodles, flavours and toppings. You can even doodle your own graphic label and pick a name before sealing it all in a balloon-like bag to take away and (hopefully) enjoy at a later date.

When evening falls, wander to the unassuming **Yoshimuraya**, the birthplace of Iekei ramen – a Yokohama original established in 1974 and known for its pork-soy broth and extra thick noodles (like jeans, noodles were also flared in the 1970s). The queue will likely be around the block, but the first sip of soup always makes the waiting feel like part of the ritual. Nearby, **Rairaiken** is a branch of the oldest ramen store in Japan (founded in Asakusa in 1910) where the noodles arrive in steaming, flavourful bowls with a side of history.

By the bay, the scents of soy and sesame drift through the air, and you realise that, here, ramen is not just food. It's the soul of the port, the steaming heart of the city's culinary culture, and every bowl tells a story.

MIURA & JOGASHIMA ISLAND

Sea air, a fresh tuna market and a jagged coastline

~65 min

~10–15 min

GETTING THERE

From Shinagawa Station, take the Keikyu Line to Misakiguchi Station (~65 min). From the main exit, local buses or taxis connect to Misaki Port (10 min) and Jogashima Island (15 min).

trip.pref.kanagawa.jp/area/miura/miura

DISCOVER

Misaki Port, tuna auctions, rugged coastlines.

SEASONAL HIGHLIGHTS

Spring: wildflowers on Jogashima Island. Autumn: best tuna season. Winter: quiet beaches, clear Fuji views across the bay.

Overnighter → *Make the most of this day trip by staying overnight and visiting the seafood market in the early morning when the tuna auctions take place. Or take the bus to Jogashima Island from Misakiguchi Station, then ferry to Misaki Port for a seafood feast. If you have time, consider combining this day trip with a visit to Mount Nokogiri (see page 154) – just a lovely 40-minute ferry trip away.*

Many people make the trek to Kamakura, but you can go beyond to **Miura**, on the southern tip of Kanagawa Prefecture, which breaks into inlets, ports and outcrops with quiet bays, fishing harbours and beaches where the wind is always tousling trees and whipping up waves.

At the southern edge of Miura sits **Misaki**, a fishing town whose name has long been tied to the sea's most powerful catch: maguro (tuna). At **Misaki Port**, the tuna auction at the **Misaki Wholesale Seafood Market** pulses with energy. The market is filled with the calls of both sellers and buyers. Harbour cafes and small restaurants serve slices of sashimi so fresh they melt on your tongue, leaving a lingering memory of the sea. The flavour is rich and almost buttery, often balanced by shiso leaf and citrus.

From Misaki, a short bus or taxi ride takes you across the bridge to **Jogashima Island**, where coastal cliffs are sculpted by centuries of waves, caves are formed by the power of the sea, and **Awasaki Lighthouse** stands watchful above the treacherous surf. Pungent kelp and sea salt flavour the air, and high above in the sky, seabirds wail mournfully. For the first few months of the year, walking paths lead past wildflowers and coastal grasses, the immense Pacific Ocean your backdrop. Yellow field mustard and Kawazu cherry blossoms provide an intense, painterly canvas. Misshapen rock formations surround Jogashima and the rugged coastline of **Nishizaki-no-Iso**. On clear days, the island features one of Japan's best 'Mount Fuji from afar' views, the majestic mountain distant but clear on the horizon with a dramatic foreground of waves crashing over angular rocks.

Inland from Misaki, you'll see rustic and rural farmland gridded by neat rows of cabbages and daikon. Roadside stands sell vegetables tugged from the soil that very morning, along with freshly picked strawberries. Surely this is what gives Miura its character – the interplay of land and sea, fishing nets drying in the sun, markets groaning with tuna and fields of planted produce stretching quiet and green.

MOUNT FUJI VIEW DAY TRIPS

Spectacular and memorable Fuji views can be found on many of the day trips in this book, including Miho Beach (see page 103), Lake Kawaguchi (see page 202) and Nihondaira Yume Terrace (see page 99). There are other iconic spots across Shizuoka where Mount Fuji reveals its many moods – from mist-shrouded mystery to crystalline winter visions. Here are some of our favourites.

OBUCHI SASABA

Travel from Shizuoka to Obuchi Sasaba tea fields (you'll need to catch a series of buses and trains that can take up to 2 hours, or hire a car if you can – it's faster). If you are there between April and May, it's tea-harvesting season. There is no picking workshop or tea house experience here; however, you'll get one of the most iconic views of Mount Fuji. In April in particular, Fuji wears a bonnet of snow and proudly looks down upon rows and rows of billowy tea terraces bowed before the mountain in gentle respect.

Getting there:

* **From Tokyo Station, take the JR Tokaido Line to Shizuoka Station, then transfer to the Minobu Line for Fujinomiya Station. Take the north exit, then catch a taxi or local bus to the tea fields (~2.5 hr).**
* **fujinomiya.gr.jp**

SEASONAL HIGHLIGHTS: → April–May for tea harvesting and snow-topped Fuji.

MIZUGATSUKA PARK

High on the slopes between forest and cloud, Mizugatsuka Park, at the edge of Fuji's base, seems to bring you close enough to touch Fuji's peak. This is not one of those distant views – the mountain is immense, its symmetry pure against the sky. On clear mornings, the peak stands aloft like a god, the perfect vision with the foreground adorned by wildflowers or, in autumn, by red leaves at the base.

Getting there:

* **From Tokyo Station, take the JR Tokaido Shinkansen to Mishima Station, then take the Tokaido and Gotemba lines to Gotemba Station. From the station's main exit, catch the Fujisan Skyline bus to Mizugatsuka Park (~2.5 hr).**
* **pref.shizuoka.jp**

SEASONAL HIGHLIGHTS: → May–June for wildflowers. October–November for autumn leaves.

MOUNT FUJI SHIZUOKA AIRPORT

Few airports have a view such as this. Beyond the runway, Mount Fuji's perfect cone rises, a watchful, protective sentinel. The glass windows of the airport frame the mountain like a painting – each hour shifting colour, the perfect way to pass the time while waiting for a flight. Every landing is a greeting; every take-off carries a quiet blessing, Fuji breathing out the wind that lifts you skyward.

Getting there:

* **From Tokyo Station, take the JR Tokaido Line to Shizuoka Station. Take the north exit, then catch a local bus to Mount Fuji Shizuoka Airport (45–60 mins).**
* **mtfuji-shizuokaairport.jp**

SEASONAL HIGHLIGHTS: → winter for the clearest Fuji views.

SURUGA BAY FERRY

The ferry glides across Suruga Bay, the water a mirror that holds Fuji's reflection like a treasure. The air smells of salt and diesel; every wave feels like a heartbeat. As the ferry moves between Shimizu and Toi, the mountain is your constant companion – sometimes veiled in mist, sometimes a vibrant white against the blue sky. Passengers lean against the railings in silence, breath stolen, time slowing to near stillness. Why not consider making the crossing to Shuzenji, Ito and Atami before returning to Tokyo?

Getting there:

* From Tokyo Station, take the JR Tokaido Shinkansen to Shizuoka Station, then transfer to the Tokaido Line for Shimizu Station. From the east exit, catch a shuttle bus to Shimizu Port (~1 hr 50 min). The ferry ride lasts about 75 minutes one way.
* 223-ferry.or.jp/en.html

SEASONAL HIGHLIGHTS: → spring and autumn for clear skies and calm waters.

CAPE OSE

A narrow peninsula curls into Suruga Bay like a natural platform, designed by a god for the sole purpose of looking at Mount Fuji. At Cape Ose, the water lies still, reflecting Fuji so precisely it feels doubled – a mountain above, an illusion below. The Ose Shrine is set in a grove of ancient camphor trees, their roots tangled in the sand. From the cape's edge, Fuji looms across the bay, a not-too-distant image with a foreground of a gently sloping mountain that makes it appear like a three-dimensional tableau.

Getting there:

* From Tokyo Station, take the JR Tokaido Shinkansen to Mishima, then change to the JR Tokaido Line for Numazu Station. Take the south exit, then catch a local bus to Osezaki (~2.5 hr).
* https://trip.numazukanko.jp

SEASONAL HIGHLIGHTS: → winter for calm waters and sharp reflections.

LAKE TANUKI

At dawn, Lake Tanuki is like glass, with Fuji glowing a faint rose colour in the first light. This is another close-up view: the observation deck gives you a vision of Fuji spread majestically out before a fringe of cedars, the mountain's reflection flawless in the water. Here is where you might get to see the famous Double Diamond Fuji, where the rising sun hits the peak and is then reflected perfectly in the water – a sparkling jewel. It's a popular camping spot, so you may not be alone when you rise from your tent at dawn to take in the almost holy stillness. In spring, cherry petals float across the surface; in autumn, the lake catches every ember of red from the trees. To see Fuji here is to witness a wonder mirrored – perfection existing both in reality and in some luminous otherworld. If you miss the sunrise, note that Lake Yamanaka features a sunset version of Double Diamond Fuji.

Getting there:

* From Tokyo Station, take the JR Tokaido Shinkansen to Mishima Station, then transfer to the Tokaido Line for Fuji Station. From Fuji Station, take the Minobu Line to Fujinomiya Station. Take the north exit, then catch a local bus to Lake Tanuki (~2.5 hr).
* https://fujinomiya.gr.jp

SEASONAL HIGHLIGHTS: → April–May for cherry blossoms or October–November for autumn colours.

SATTA PASS

Above the Old Tokaido Road, Satta Pass gently winds through tea fields and pines that overlook the sea. This is where artist Hiroshige once painted his famous Fuji views. The scent of citrus drifts from the groves, and cicadas sing in the wind. Travellers pause at the lookout to take in a rare sight: Fuji, the ocean and a multi-level, chaotic highway. This is nature and human-made, the modern and the ancient, merging together in an expertly arranged montage that Hiroshige could never have predicted.

Getting there:

* From Tokyo Station, take the JR Tokaido Line to Yui Station (~2 hr). From the main exit, walk or take a taxi to the Satta Pass viewpoint.
* https://shizuoka-guide.com

SEASONAL HIGHLIGHTS: → winter for crystal-clear coastal views.

SHIMOYOSHIDA HONCHO STREET

One of the most iconic views of the mountain: on Honcho Street in Shimoyoshida, Mount Fuji rises at the end of a quiet shopping lane lined with lanterns, street signs, telephone poles and low rooftops. The mountain looms so large, it almost feels like you could reach out and touch it – an incredibly picturesque and cinematic image.

Getting there:

* From Tokyo Station, take the JR Chuo Line to Otsuki Station, the transfer to the Fujikyu Line for Shimoyoshida Station (~2 hr 15 min). From the main exit, walk 5 minutes to Honcho Street.
* https://fujisan.ne.jp

SEASONAL HIGHLIGHTS: → April for cherry blossoms. November for clear skies.

FUJIMI KOTOKU KOEN

A serene hillside park near Fujiyoshida, Fujimi Kotoku Koen frames Fuji behind seasonal leaves and old stone lanterns and statues. In spring, azaleas and blossoms ignite the slopes; in autumn, golden ginkgo leaves show off the peak beautifully.

Getting there:

* From Tokyo Station, take the JR Chuo Line to Otsuki, then the Fujikyu Line to Fujisan Station (~2.5 hr). Take the main exit, then catch a local bus or walk for 20 minutes to the park.
* www.city.fujiyoshida.yamanashi.jp

SEASONAL HIGHLIGHTS: → October–November for autumn colours and clear air.

NOSON KOEN

Noson Koen is a peaceful local park on the gentle plains near Mount Fuji, where farmers' fields stretch towards the mountain. It's beloved by locals for its wide lawns, cherry trees and view of Fuji's immense form framed by open sky. Spring brings a haze of pink petals drifting across green rice shoots. The shot you want to get here, however, is towering Fuji against a backdrop of agrarian fields and, in the foreground, Fuji's reflection in the crystalline waters.

Getting there:

* From Tokyo Station, take the JR Chuo Line to Otsuki Station, then transfer to the Fujikyu Line for Fujisan Station (~2.5 hr). From the main exit, it's a short walk or taxi ride to the park.
* https://fujiyoshida.net/en/see-and-do/40

SEASONAL HIGHLIGHTS: → April–May for cherry blossoms and spring greenery.

EAST

As you head east, Tokyo softens into river towns, tidal flats and quiet neighbourhoods edged by the wide, slow sweep of the Tone and Edo rivers. Here, the air tastes faintly of salt and reeds, and the horizon opens into lowlands rich with folklore, shrines and Edo-period echoes. The east has a gentleness – bamboo groves whispering along canals, tiny museums full of local history, and old merchants' streets lined with sweet shops and soy breweries. You can wander through fishing villages along the bay, cycle floodplains alive with herons, or step through the lantern-lit gates of ancient shrines that once guided travellers to safety. Further from Tokyo, it's all about the ocean – the jagged coastlines and broad seas of the Boso Peninsula, early morning fish catches and rocks shaped by centuries of tide and wind. Day trips eastward feel like travels into a gentler Japan – one of waterways, wind patterns and small communities that hold on to the deeply human pace of the past and live by the changing tides of the sea.

KAMOGAWA, P 163

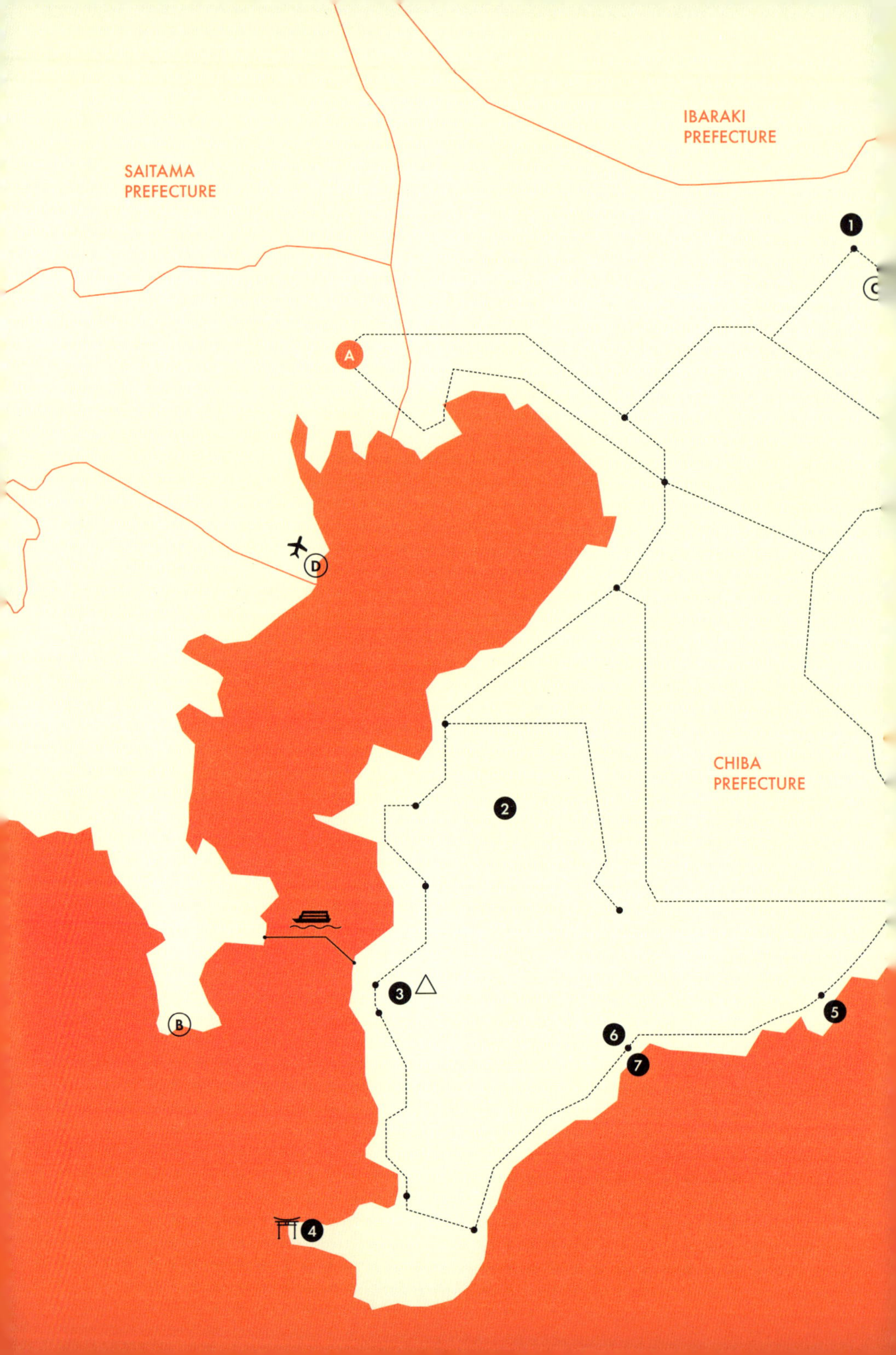
IBARAKI
PREFECTURE
SAITAMA
PREFECTURE
CHIBA
PREFECTURE
A
B
C
D
1
2
3
4
5
6
7

EAST DAY TRIPS

1. The Temple Town of Narita
2. Kurkku Fields
3. Mount Nokogiri
4. Sunosaki Shrine
5. Breezy Katsuura
6. Coastal Kamogawa
7. Kamogawa Onsen
8. Kikkoman Soy Sauce Factory & Museum

KEY

- (A) Tokyo
- (B) Miura
- (C) Narita Airport
- (D) Haneda Airport
- •---• Local Train Routes
- •—• Ferry Routes

Overnighter & Weekender Ideas

→ Kurkku Fields, Mount Nokogiri & Miura *(see page 139)*

→ Sunosaki Shrine, Mount Nokogiri & Kurkku Fields

→ Katsuura & Kamogawa

THE TEMPLE TOWN OF NARITA

Surprisingly spectacular temple grounds and retro streets near the airport

1 hr

GETTING THERE

From Tokyo Station, take the JR Sobu Line to Narita Station (1 hr). Take the east exit.

naritasan.or.jp

DISCOVER

Naritasan Shinsho-ji Temple, Naritasan Omotesando Street, Great Pagoda of Peace, unagi restaurants.

SEASONAL HIGHLIGHTS

Spring: cherry blossoms. Autumn: crimson foliage in Naritasan Park. New Year: temple festivities.

Advice → *Travellers often spend the last night of their Japan trip in Narita before an early flight from Narita International Airport. If that's you, make the most of it by staying in one of the town's stylish ryokan or onsen hotels. Get to the town early to experience the temple before the crowds, or take a night stroll through the grounds – it's very atmospheric. Enjoy unagi at Kawatoyo or Surugaya. Check festival dates before visiting.*

It would be fair to assume that Narita is just a waiting room between worlds, an airport town offering you a convenient stop near one of the world's busiest airports. Yet it's so much more. Just 10 minutes from the terminal, the scents of cedar, incense and soy drift on the air and suddenly you are walking through history. **Narita Town** reveals itself like a centuries-old secret – a place where pilgrims once walked and temple bells still toll above tiled rooftops.

Wander down **Narita Omotesando**, the old approach road – almost a kilometre of Edo nostalgia. Lanterns swing in the breeze, and the scent of grilled unagi rises from open-fronted restaurants where chefs have tended the same fires for two centuries. Ceramics shops, calligraphy studios and wagashi confectioners line the way. Each doorway is a small time machine, each shopkeeper's bow a bridge between eras.

The **Naritasan Shinsho-ji Temple** is the town's heart – a vast, breathing complex founded over a thousand years ago. Its grand gates rise before you, dark wood gleaming with the touch of countless hands. Pass through incense smoke curling in slow devotion, and enter a world of carvings, pagodas and soft chanting. The temple and its surrounds are spectacular and easily rival Kyoto's finest. Dedicated to Shingon Buddhist teachings, Naritasan is a beacon of stillness. Inside, look into the fierce gaze of **Fudo Myo-o**, the Buddhist king of wisdom (carved by revered monk Kobo Daishi, or Kukai, himself).

On festival days, sumo wrestlers and actors gather here to scatter beans for good fortune, and at New Year, millions pour through the temple gates – the air alive with prayer and promise. You might find quieter joy collecting **Goshuin** temple stamps, each a brushstroke of beauty and blessing.

It's such an unexpected pleasure to have a day strolling throughout Tokyo's rich history before you fly out or after you fly in, the memory settling in your soul, leaving an infinite sense of calm.

成田山
開運だるま
成田山
開運だるま

出世稲荷
出世
開運
商売
繁昌
大本山 成田山

令和８年　成田山初詣
謹　賀　新　年
順路
順路

KURKKU FIELDS

An art field and memorable library on a sustainable farm

~90 min (bus)
OR
77 min (train)
20 min (taxi)

GETTING THERE

From Tokyo Station Yaesu Bus Terminal, take a direct highway bus (~90 min) to Kurkku Fields Iriguchi Bus Stop in Kisarazu City. Or, from Tokyo Station, take the JR Uchibo Line to Kisarazu Station (77 min), then catch a taxi to Kurkku Fields (20 min).

kurkkufields.jp

DISCOVER

Organic farm and free-range dairy, outdoor artworks including works by Yayoi Kusama, the Library in the Earth.

SEASONAL HIGHLIGHTS

Spring and summer: milky-green fields, active farm life. Autumn: harvest time, richer light, art against golden hills.

Advice → *Entry is free. Bring your walking shoes, time and curiosity. Visit on weekdays or early mornings for a quieter experience.*

Weekender → *Expand this day trip into a weekend away by combining it with Mount Nokogiri (see page 154) and Miura (see page 139).*

Ninety minutes from Tokyo, a stretch of reclaimed pasture rises from the fringe of suburbia and morphs into something special. **Kurkku Fields** is both a farm and an art park. More than that, however, it is an experiment in living softly, in merging the life-affirming joys of art and agriculture, in designing a future of sustainability and believing.

As you walk between rows of heirloom vegetables (and free-roaming buffalo), solar panels hum benevolently. Dotted among the open fields you'll find artworks that seem to have grown organically from the soil, nurtured by possibility. At the edge of a meadow you'll see a work by Yayoi Kusama, *Guidepost to the New World* – polka-dotted lumps, blobs and tentacles half-submerged in a pond. One of Kusama's infinity rooms can also be found on the grounds, along with works by Sebastian Masuda (such as *Gaping Hole Secret*), David Hockney, Anish Kapoor and more.

Inside the underground **Library in the Earth**, walls of recycled cork hold shelves with books on food, soil, ecology, poetry and art. Hiroshi Nakamura and NAP Architects created the space to feel like a natural part of the landscape. Undulating walls are overgrown with plants. Inside, curved walkways circle the library. A circlet of shelves holds up a high, spiralling roof with a porthole to the sky, muted light diffusing into the room creating a sacred air. On the dining terrace newly grown vegetables are served with freshly collected eggs – the taste is simple, every dish echoing connection with the land.

There is also accommodation here, and the **Cocoon Villas** are worth viewing: wooden pods interlaced with winding paths and overgrown with abundant foliage – they look like remnants of a past, or possibly a future, utopian society.

Fields glow gold as light slowly fades. The air smells of hay and new growth. Art stands among stalks of green, cows graze near sculptures, the library's rooftop curves upwards. Kurkku Fields doesn't just show what sustainability *can* be; it shows what it *is*: a slow gathering of acts – a farm, a work of art, a library underground – all tended, created and grown with care.

MOUNT NOKOGIRI

A dragon mountain, a view of Hell and the goddess of mercy, all by ferry

Train	90 min
Bus	12 min
Ferry	40 min
Walk	10 min

GETTING THERE

From Tokyo Station, take the Yokosuka Line to Kurihama Station (90 min), then catch the bus to Kurihama Port (12 min). Hop on the Tokyo Wan Ferry to Kanaya Port, a 40-minute crossing of Tokyo Bay with sweeping views of the peninsula. From Kanaya Port, it's a 10-minute walk to the Nokogiriyama Ropeway or trailhead.

mt-nokogiri.co.jp

DISCOVER

Nihon-ji Temple and its giant Yakushi Nyorai Buddha, Hyaku-Shaku Kannon, Jigoku Nozoki ('View of Hell') cliff lookout, 1500 Arhat statues scattered through the forest.

SEASONAL HIGHLIGHTS

Spring: sakura, narcissus.
Autumn: striking maples.
Winter: clear days for Fuji views.

Advice → *If you get seasick and prefer to catch the train, you can go from Tokyo Station to Hama-Kanaya Station in 2 hours 15 minutes.*

Weekender → *Expand this day trip into a weekend away by combining it with Miura (see page 139) and Kurkku Fields (see page 153).*

The ferry pulls lazily out from **Kurihama**, carrying you across Tokyo Bay, where gulls circle in the salt wind, the city's skyline fading to distant blue haze. High above the coast ahead rises **Nokogiriyama** – Mount Nokogiri or 'Saw Mountain' – its jagged ridges shaped like saw-tooth edges ... or the back of a dozing dragon.

Landing at **Kanaya Port**, you can ascend by ropeway or climb on foot through cedar trees and stone steps once trodden by monks. You'll find something special around every bend, something carved by time or hewn from the rock with sacred hands – this is a mountain sculpted by faith, where **Nihon-ji Temple** sits in deep, devoted repose.

Above you, the vast **Yakushi Nyorai**, Buddha of Healing, towers 31 metres (101 feet) high – carved into the mountain in 1783 by master stonemason Jin Nishimura. The gaze is quiet, tranquil and somehow infinite, the face weathered smooth by centuries of coastal elements. Around the sculpture lie hundreds of **Arhat statues**, each with a unique expression – laughter, sorrow, peace – the faces of the deeply spiritual ones who moved beyond the teachings and into true enlightenment. Further along the ridge, the **Hyaku-Shaku Kannon** appears, a 30-metre (98-feet) goddess carved into the cliff in 1966, her features serene against the coarse stone.

Heading south, the path opens suddenly to **Jigoku Nozoki**, the 'View of Hell'. A narrow ledge juts out into the sky, the bay spread out below like a restless mirror. Standing there, clouds beneath your feet, you feel the paradox of the mountain – fear and awe in equal measure, the sacred and the natural dancing on the edge of the abyss.

If you have time, this area has many treasures. Five kilometres (3 miles) to the south, Kyonan's **Narcissus Road** blooms early, vibrant whites and yellows covering the slopes. To the north is **Kimitsu**; here, you'll find the famous **Nomizo Falls**, where a stone arch, **Kameiwa Cave**, frames the forest, the small waterfall running through it. As the morning light slants through the gap, it turns the pool a golden colour. At certain times of the year, the light reflects off the water at a specific angle, transforming the arch and its reflection into a love heart glowing with light.

SUNOSAKI SHRINE

Tides, torii and matchmaking at the sea's edge

———	Train	~1 hr 50 min
········	Bus	~30 min
- - - -	Walk	3 min

GETTING THERE

From Tokyo Station, take the JR Uchibo Line to Tateyama Station (~1 hr 50 min). From the east exit, board the JR Kanto bus Sunosaki Line to Susaki Jinja-mae (~30 min), then walk 3 minutes to the shrine.

tateyamacity.com/en/shrines-temples/sunosaki-shrine

DISCOVER

The coastal Hama-torii, Yakubarai Saka staircase, sunset over the Pacific.

SEASONAL HIGHLIGHTS

Summer: festival days (20–21 August) for vibrant rituals and lanterns. Winter: clearing weather, sharp Fuji sightings.

Advice → *Check the tides and horizon visibility – Fuji appears only on very clear days. Late afternoon and sunset offer the best light for the torii and ocean views. There are fewer crowds in the evening, so linger until after the last glows fade.*

Weekender → *Expand this day trip into a weekend away by combining it with Kurkku Fields (see page 152) and Mount Nokogiri (see page 154).*

From the Boso Peninsula, **Sunosaki Shrine** gazes out across the vast ocean to where sea and sky meet, the coastal wind carrying salt and the crash of waves. The **Goshinseki torii** at the shore stands sentinel, framing a world of light, ocean, rocks. Generations of voyagers, warriors and couples have stood here, eyes cast to the horizon, hearts ready for transition and renewal. Further up, another torii gate frames a distant, ponderous Mount Fuji.

One of the legends of the shrine tells of 12th-century samurai and shogun Minamoto no Yoritomo landing nearby after defeat, seeking blessing and second chances. Beneath the vermillion gates and along the forested path, visitors come for the same blessings, for successful matchmaking, safe voyages and the promise that the sea will deliver their wishes. If it has already worked out for you, ring the **Bell of Happiness**.

Climb the 150 stone steps up the hillside to the entrance of the shrine's main hall. At the top, the view opens to the blue sea, the torii silently waiting like a gate to a new world and, in the distance, a shadow space of ridges and further shores where Fuji sometimes shows its crown.

The scene shifts with the setting sun, the torii becoming a silhouette against coral sky. The sea quietens. Perhaps offer your own prayers for moments of renewal and connection, for what is and what could be. The shrine lanterns gently come to life, glowing like a hearth fire. In the stillness of the enfolding evening, the torii gate frames a new horizon.

BREEZY KATSUURA

A seafood market ritual edged by wild cliffs over the vast Pacific Ocean

~2 hr
OR
2.5 hr

GETTING THERE
From Tokyo Station, take the Limited Express Wakashio to Katsuura Station (~2 hr). Take the east exit. Or take the bus from Tokyo Station Yaesu Bus Terminal to Kusoku Budai Iriguchi (2.5 hr).

city.katsuura.lg.jp

DISCOVER
Katsuura Morning Market, Ubara Utopia coastal hiking trail, Tomisaki Shrine, Hina Matsuri doll festival, local beaches and onsen ryokan along the Pacific coast.

SEASONAL HIGHLIGHTS
Spring: Hina Matsuri doll festival (March). Summer: swimming, sashimi, seaside festivals, snorkelling, fireworks. Autumn: quieter with mild weather, clear ocean views, golden sunsets. Winter: kinmedai season, bracing coastal walks.

Advice → *Start your day trip early (really early) to get to the morning market. Wear good shoes for Ubara cliffs. Don't leave without trying the kinmedai sashimi.*

Weekender → *Expand this day trip into a weekend away by combining it with Coastal Kamogawa* *(see page 162)* *and Kamogawa Onsen* *(see page 164).*

Katsuura is a town that moves to the rhythm of the tide. Long before the sun peeks over the Pacific, while gulls begin their silver arcs and Tokyo still dreams, lanterns flicker to life in the narrow lanes of the **Katsuura Morning Market** (daily, from dawn to around 11 am). Both farm-to-table and sea-to-table, the market stalls spill over with glistening seaweed, giant daikon and mandarins glowing like tiny suns. This is not just a morning market; it's a dawn ritual. Everyone is here for the morning's catch – hauled from the sea, impossibly fresh.

This market – one of Japan's 'big three' alongside Takayama and Wajima – has been trading for more than 400 years, and you can feel every century in the creak of wooden stalls and the easy rhythm of the locals. Eighty-odd stands stretch up from the harbour along **Asaichi-dori**, each one a chapter in the ocean's story. The fish here come straight from Katsuura's nine ports: tuna, yellowtail, sardines and the prized kinmedai (golden-eye snapper). In winter, this fish stars in steaming hotpots; in summer, it gleams on ice as ruby-red sashimi.

Step away from the bustle, and the Pacific roars at your feet. Katsuura's coastline is all theatre – carved cliffs, echoing caves and waves that crash dramatically against the rocks. **Ubara Utopia**, a local hiking trail, winds through this wild scene of sea and sky, where every corner reveals another heart-thumping vista.

East of the bay near Ubara Station, the **Katsuura Marine Park Underwater Observation Tower** features a tower 60 metres (197 feet) from the shore from where you can watch the power of the waves or descend 8 metres (26 feet) below the water to observe ocean creatures in their natural habitat.

Above town, the **Tomisaki Shrine** watches over everything. In February and March, the steps are transformed, coloured with hundreds of hina dolls for the annual **Hina Matsuri** festival. The long, red-carpeted stairs feature an estimated 1800 dolls, one of Japan's most spectacular doll displays.

Katsuura is just a couple of hours from Tokyo, but it feels like another realm – one ruled by tides, time and the scent of soy and salt. If you want a relaxing break from the city, stay overnight in a seaside ryokan, soak in an onsen with views of the endless blue, and wake to grilled fish and miso soup as the waves tumble below. At night, that same sound seeps through the shoji screens, a blissful reminder of Katsuura's deep connection with the sea and the seasons.

¥650

COASTAL KAMOGAWA

The sea, fresh seafood, rice terraces and a forest shrine

~2 hr

OR

2.5 hr

GETTING THERE

From Tokyo Station, take the Limited Express Wakashio to Awa-Kamogawa Station (~2 hr. Take the east exit. Or take the bus from Tokyo Station Yaesu Bus Terminal to Kameda Byoin. (2.5 hr).

city.kamogawa.lg.jp

DISCOVER

Maebara Beach, Kamogawa Sea World, Oyama Senmaida rice terraces (especially the autumn light-up), Seicho-ji Temple.

SEASONAL HIGHLIGHTS

Spring: wildflowers along the coast. Summer: swimming, seaside activity. Autumn: rice terrace light-up, crisp sea breezes.

Advice → *Kamogawa's Sea World is one of the Chiba region's most popular attractions, an expansive marine park at the water's edge that features a host of aquatic life.*

Weekender → *Expand this day trip into a weekend away by combining it with Kamogawa Onsen (see page 164) and Katsuura (see page 158).*

The coastal town of **Kamogawa** is perched on the eastern edge of the Boso Peninsula, where the Pacific gently rolls onto the shore. Kamogawa has always been bound to the sea – the ocean a potent symbol shaping both the town's spirit and its economy. Fishing boats set out each dawn, and seafood markets throng with visitors buying the freshest tuna, squid and flounder pulled straight from the depths. Many small seafood markets and eateries dot the landscape, selling the ocean's bounty.

Maebara Beach is a long stretch of golden sand, perfect for a stroll in the glow of sunset, while **Niemonjima**, a rocky island just offshore, can be viewed from a small ferry. Glass-bottom boats gaze down at forests of seaweed dancing in the underwater light. In spring, wildflowers colour the shoreline.

The inland hills are famous for their rice paddies and terraced fields. The **Oyama Senmaida** rice terraces – one of Japan's few surviving rain-fed terraced paddies – starkly mirror the clouds above. During autumn, the fields are illuminated by thousands of tiny lanterns, fireflies blinking in the enfolding dark.

The **Seicho-ji Temple** lies further inland, hidden in forests of cedar. It was founded in 771 CE by a priest, Fushigi Hoshi, and it's famous as the place where the Buddhist reformer Nichiren first declared his teachings. A large cedar, the **sennen-sugi** (1000-year tree) is considered the second-tallest cedar in Japan. There is a shukubo (lodging) at the temple, and it's worth staying over as the vista from the temple down to the Pacific Ocean is dramatic – sky, sea and eternity blended into one of Japan's 'Top 100 Sunrise Views'. Or stay in seaside ryokan where sliding doors open and frame the waves.

Seafood not to miss in Kamogawa includes kinmedai (golden-eye snapper), ayu (sweetfish) and the freshest sashimi. Farmers' markets also offer the region's mandarins and loquats, as well as fresh rice crackers toasted on an open flame.

Here, between sea and song, Kamogawa moves slowly. It reminds you that Japan is more than cities and shrines – it is also waves against sand, a farmer's field, a fisherman's boat, a lantern glowing above the rice. To visit Kamogawa is to let the Pacific wash the noise away, until only the rhythms of tide and heart remain.

KAMOGAWA ONSEN

A seaside day-bathing escape

~2 hr
OR
2.5 hr
+
~4 min

GETTING THERE

From Tokyo Station, take the Limited Express Wakashio to Awa-Kamogawa Station (~2 hr). Take the east exit. Or take the bus from Tokyo Station Yaesu Bus Terminal to Kameda Byoin (2.5 hr). For some onsen along the coast, transfer to the Uchibo Line for Futomi Station (~4 min).

visitkamogawa.com

DISCOVER

Kamogawakan, Onsen Puro HARUKA, Kamogawa Grand Hotel – Spa Gallery Uminokairo, Ezawakan, Boso Kamogawa Hot Springs Zekuu.

SEASONAL HIGHLIGHTS

Spring: early cherry blossoms.
Winter: milder coastal climate.

Advice → *Many Kamogawa onsen ryokan offer day bathing on weekends, often late morning to afternoon and again in the evening. Hours and tattoo policies vary – always check ahead. Pick up a detailed map of day-bathing facilities at the Awa-Kamogawa Station Tourist Information Centre.*

Weekender → *Expand this day trip into a weekend away by combining it with Coastal Kamogawa (see page 162) and Katsuura (see page 158).*

The **Kamogawa coast** on the Boso Peninsula is geothermally blessed, with around 20 day-use onsen scattered along the shoreline providing a deeply restorative (and possibly much-needed) mini-break from Tokyo. The comfortable, reservation-only Wakashio train delivers you straight from the city to the sea, where mineral-rich waters meet wide horizons.

Kamogawa's appeal lies in its balance: the deep blue of the Pacific unfurling to the east; rocky coves and beaches below; and forests, rice terraces and hills rising to the west. Steam curls from baths as waves roll in, the ocean and onsen breathing together. Many facilities offer onsite dining, making it easy to fall into a gentle rhythm of soak, eat, rest, repeat. Arrive early and you can even onsen-hop, as each bath offers a distinct mood, view and mineral profile.

Awa-Kamogawa and Futomi stations act as gateways to your bathing day. **Kamogawakan**, about 7 minutes by taxi from Awa-Kamogawa Station, offers a more luxurious day-bathing experience. Its salt-rich waters include the rooftop **Onsen Puro HARUKA**, with expansive Pacific views. This mixed-gender bath uses special garments so families and friends can bathe together; check details online.

A short walk from Awa-Kamogawa Station, **Kamogawa Grand Hotel – Spa Gallery Uminokairo** features multiple baths, including a stone-lined rotenburo (outdoor bath) overlooking the ocean, plus private baths for an extra fee. Day-bathing hours are limited and vary by day, so confirm ahead.

For an onsen with a bit of history, **Ezawakan**, a 10-minute taxi ride from Awa-Kamogawa Station or an 11-minute walk from Futomi Station, dates back to the early 20th century. Favoured by artists such as Sotaro Yasui, it offers a rustic soak and the **Ozashiki Gallery**, where seafood lunches are served amid artworks. Reservations are required.

Finally, **Boso Kamogawa Hot Springs Zekuu**, a 15-minute walk from Futomi Station, offers seaside baths where rocky enclaves frame a sparkling horizon, alongside private and public options.

KIKKOMAN SOY SAUCE FACTORY & MUSEUM

An homage to one of the world's great condiments

——	Train	~30 min
═══	Train	~20 min
- - - - -	Walk	5 min

GETTING THERE

From Tokyo Station, take the Tokiwa Limited express to Kashiwa Station (~30 min), then transfer to the Tobu Urban Park Line for Noda-shi Station (~20 min). The museum is a 5-minute walk from the station's east exit.

kikkoman.co.jp

DISCOVER

Kikkoman Soy Sauce Factory and Museum, factory tours, Tone River walk, old merchant houses.

SEASONAL HIGHLIGHTS

Soy sauce is good at all times.

Advice → *Advance online reservations are required for the factory tour, available for groups of two or more people. Tours run Mondays–Fridays, except on national holidays and other unscheduled holidays.*

Tours (in English and Mandarin Chinese) are generally self-guided with audio headsets.

Bring a small bag – the gift shop will test your willpower.

While in the Chiba region, don't forget to try the food specialties: namero (minced fish with miso), futomaki (hand rolls with colourful patterns in the centre) and peanuts.

You might come to **Noda** expecting a quiet riverside town – and that's exactly what it is. Quiet, yes, but steeped (and steeping) in something deliciously deep and dark. Once, the **Tone-gawa River** ferried barges full of goods to Edo; today, Noda still hums faintly with that same industrious spirit – only now it smells like soy sauce. Because here, in this unassuming town, the legend of Kikkoman was born.

As your train rattles east through barley fields, you'll note the air begins to smell faintly savoury, as though the whole landscape has been marinating for centuries. A short stroll from Noda-shi Station and there it is – the **Kikkoman Soy Sauce Factory and Museum** – a place where culinary history bubbles away like poetry in a vat. Inside, time itself feels fermented. The aroma is unmistakable: salty, sweet, tangy and oddly comforting – the scent of dinner tables around the world.

Soy sauce, as you'll learn during the factory tour, is not just a condiment. It's a slow, patient alchemy of soybeans, wheat, water and salt, aged until the brew becomes symphonic. Old cedar barrels line the halls beside gleaming modern tanks – Edo meets industry in a heady waft of nostalgia. Wander through exhibits of grain sacks, black-and-white photos of workers and 18th-century prints of merchant boats stacked with barrels bound for Edo. A single thread ties it all together: humans have been obsessed with umami for a very long time.

After the tour comes the tasting – the pilgrimage fulfilled. Tiny cups of Kikkoman are poured like sacred shots. Smoky. Sugary. Deep. Possibly life-changing. And then comes the kicker: soy sauce ice cream – a soft-serve miracle that manages to be salty, sweet and surprising all at once.

In Noda, everything feels aged to perfection. Maybe it's dramatic to say soy sauce runs through the town's veins ... but the essence of the town is certainly brewed and bottled.

WEST

West of Tokyo, the land rises – first in ripples, then in peaks. Mountains call from the horizon, blue-green and regal, layered like folding screens. Within an hour, the city loosens its grip and gives way to cedar forests, river gorges, pilgrim paths, ancient temple precincts tucked high in the hills and – watching over it all with defiant splendour – a majestic Mount Fuji. This is hiking country, Kannon country, wine and sake country. It's the home of post towns and old postal roads, memorable onsen, famed bathing monkeys and architectural pilgrimages. The rivers run clear and cold, perfect for summer swims; in autumn, maples blaze along ravines; in winter, low light glows through frost-silvered pines. Ultimately, though, it is the mountains that will draw you here, spectacular peaks standing guard, like sentinels, over a distant Tokyo.

JIGOKUDANI, P 180

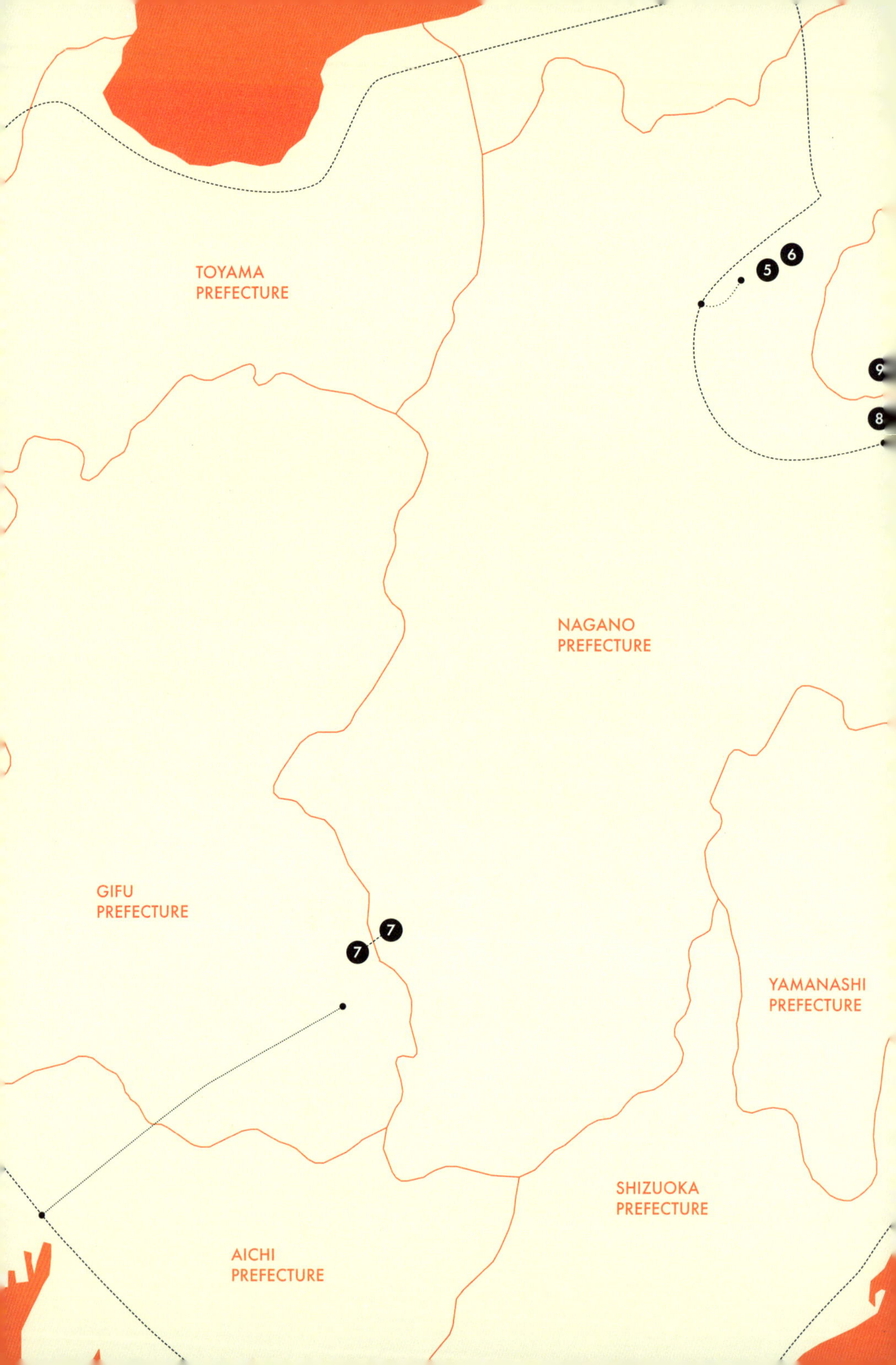
TOYAMA
PREFECTURE
NAGANO
PREFECTURE
GIFU
PREFECTURE
YAMANASHI
PREFECTURE
SHIZUOKA
PREFECTURE
AICHI
PREFECTURE
5
6
9
8
7
7

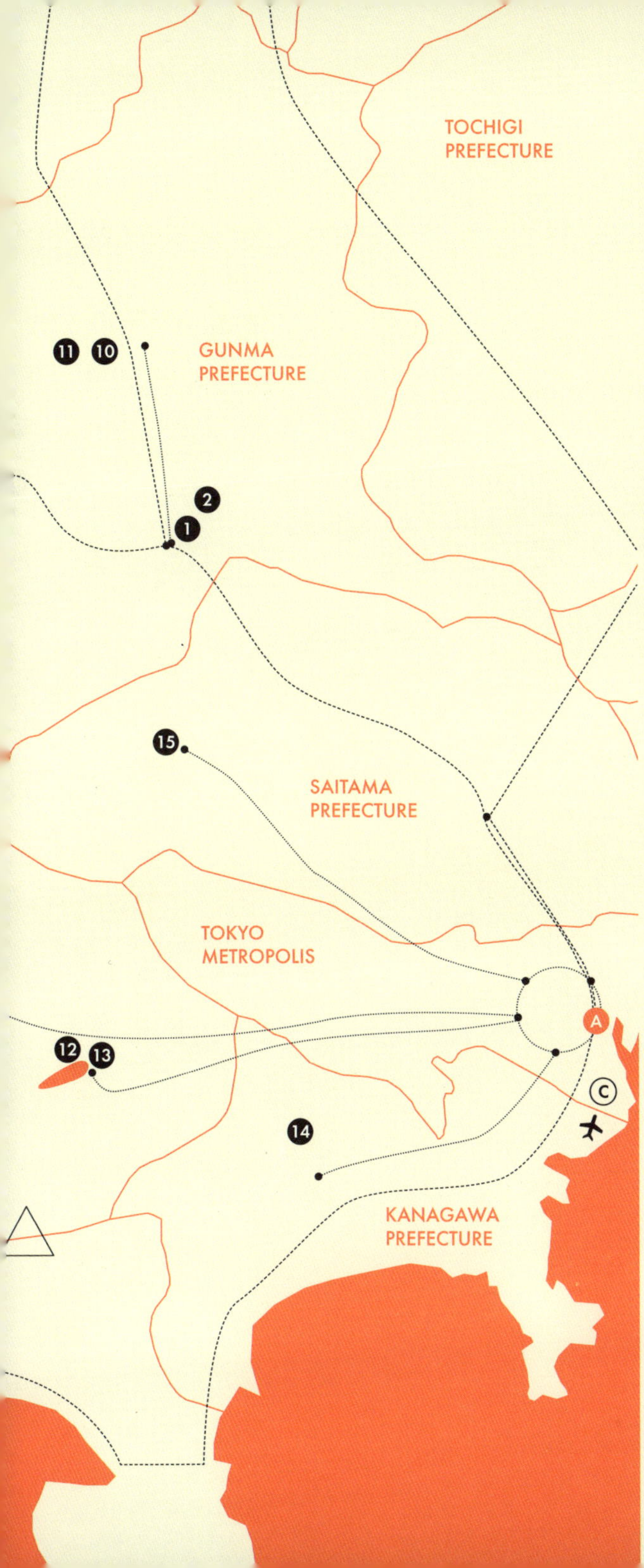

WEST DAY TRIPS

1. Daruma dolls in Takasaki
2. Merciful Takasaki
3. evam eva yamanashi
4. Yamanashi Wineries and Kofu
5. The Steaming Valley of Jigokudani
6. Shibu Onsen
7. The Nakasendo: Magome to Tsumago
8. Holy Karuizawa
9. Kusatsu Onsen
10. Hara Museum ARC
11. Ikaho Onsen
12. Kubota Itchiku Art Museum
13. Lake Kawaguchi
14. Mount Oyama
15. Adventures in Chichibu

KEY

- A Tokyo
- C Haneda Airport
- Shinkansen Routes
- Local Train Routes
- △ Mount Fuji

Overnighter & Weekender Ideas

- → *Takasaki*
- → *evam eva yamanashi, Yamanashi Wineries & Kofu*
- → *Jigokudani & Shibu Onsen*
- → *The Nakasendo: Magome to Tsumago*
- → *Hara Museum ARC & Ikaho Onsen*
- → *Kubota Itchiku Art Museum & Lake Kawaguchi*
- → *Chichibu & local walks*

DARUMA DOLLS IN TAKASAKI

Wishes, luck and Daruma history in an unassuming hub city

50 min

GETTING THERE

From Tokyo Station, take the Hokuriku or Joetsu Shinkansen to Takasaki Station (50 min). Take the west exit for local buses and taxis.

city.takasaki.gunma.jp

DISCOVER

Shorinzan Daruma-ji Temple, Daimonya Daruma Workshop.

SEASONAL HIGHLIGHTS

Spring: cherry blossoms around Mount Haruna. Autumn: temple grounds shimmer with colour. Winter: Daruma Market (January) with more than 400 stalls of good luck and red cheer.

Overnighter → *Consider making this an overnight trip to explore more of Takasaki (see page 174).*

Takasaki might seem like a pit stop on the bullet train map – a convenient transport hub between Tokyo and the mountains of Gunma, or Niigata's snow country beyond. But step out of the train station and you'll quickly discover that this city has soul, charm and a touch of eccentric magic – not least because it's home to one of Japan's most beloved icons: the Daruma doll.

These plump, wide-eyed little monks – inspired by Bodhidharma, the founder of Zen Buddhism – are equal parts spiritual guide and comical cuteness. They wobble but never fall, grinning (or scowling) their encouragement as you set your goals. The ritual is simple: paint in one blank eye when you make a wish and the other when you've achieved it. Daruma are about resilience – the art of falling down seven times and standing up eight.

In Takasaki, you can't turn a corner without bumping into one. The station gift shop bursts with Daruma-shaped snacks, Daruma tea cups, Daruma keychains and even a Daruma-shaped ekiben, or train lunch box.

But for the true believers, there's only one pilgrimage worth making: the **Shorinzan Daruma-ji Temple**, the birthplace of the Daruma itself. From Takasaki Station, hop on the Shin-Etsu Line to Gunma-Yawata Station – just one stop away – and you'll find yourself face-to-face with a gloriously retro temple sign shaped like a Daruma. Climb the steep stone steps to reach the wooden temple, built in 1697. Its walkways are filled with hundreds of Daruma dolls watching you with their unpainted gaze. To the left of the temple, a small museum shows vintage Daruma, their red shells burnished with decades of devotion. There are also places at the temple where you can buy Daruma that come with blank eyes and with a special wish scroll hidden in their prodigious bellies.

For collectors and dreamers alike, **Daimonya** – run by Nakada Sumikazu, a fifth-generation Daruma craftsman – is just a couple of minutes away across the Hanadaka Bridge and is an absolute must. Here, you can watch these talismans being carved and hand-painted with fierce brows and hopeful bellies. Daimonya's Daruma are famous for their personality – each face is slightly different, a reminder that perseverance wears many expressions. Sign up for a class where you can paint your own doll, before making your secret wish.

As you leave, you'll feel the spirit of the city: unshakable, optimistic, robust and a little rotund, just like the Daruma itself.

MERCIFUL TAKASAKI

A striking statue, an atmospheric cave, a beautiful garden and plentiful pasta

50 min

~25 min

GETTING THERE

From Tokyo Station, take the Hokuriku or Joetsu Shinkansen to Takasaki Station (50 min). From the west exit, catch Bus 8 to Kannon-Yama Park (~25 min).

city.takasaki.gunma.jp

DISCOVER

Byakue Dai-Kannon, Dokutsu-kannon, Tokumei-en Garden.

SEASONAL HIGHLIGHTS

Spring: blossoms. Summer: lush greenery, shaded garden walks. Autumn: fiery maples in Tokumei-en. Winter: frosted hills, clear mountain views.

Advice → *The regional vending machines in Takasaki have many delights and are alone worth the trip. Don't miss the local apple soda, also from a vending machine – it's sharp, sweet and delicious.*

Overnighter → *Consider making this an overnight trip by combining it with the Shorinzan Daruma-ji Temple and its famed Daruma dolls* *(see page 173).*

You'll see her first from the train – a gleaming white figure rising above the city, serene yet commanding. The **Byakue Dai-Kannon**, the Great White Goddess of Mercy, watches over **Takasaki** like a guardian spirit. At 41 metres (135 feet) tall, she's impossible to ignore, her pale robes catching the light, her calm expression turned eternally towards the mountains. When you finally stand at her feet, you will feel tiny, as though you've stumbled into a myth.

Inside, the statue becomes a quiet temple. Climb the spiral staircase through her hollow core, pausing to gaze out of narrow windows in her chest at the city unfolding below – the red temple roofs, the undulating hills and the sea of green that is **Kannon-Yama Miharashi-Dai Park**. It's easy to believe that she really does keep watch, her silent compassion stretching over Takasaki's streets.

A short walk downhill brings you to another marvel – **Dokutsu-kannon**, the Cave of the Kannon, a dim, echoing tunnel filled with 39 carved statues of the Buddha and Kannon, flickering in low light like apparitions. The air is cool and smells faintly of stone and incense. On emerging into daylight again, head to the nearby **Tokumei-en Garden**, a valley of still ponds and arched bridges. It's vast – nearly 2 hectares (5 acres) – but intimate in feeling, a masterpiece of changing seasons. In autumn, the trees blaze crimson. In spring, camellias scatter petals across the moss. Even in winter, the landscape feels alive, breathing softly beneath a dusting of frost.

After all this beauty, hunger will no doubt strike – as it inevitably does in Japan. Takasaki, surprisingly, is pasta country. When we visited, we ducked into a small trattoria near the station and were served mountainous bowls of spaghetti swimming in rich tomato sauce. It was gloriously over the top, and somehow exactly what we needed. Steve also insisted on trying the local miso katsu – a golden-fried pork cutlet drenched in dark, sweet miso. It was rich, comforting and wildly addictive.

Takasaki isn't flashy or hurried. It doesn't beg for your attention. But that's its charm – a city both humble and holy, watched over by mercy, yet fed by pasta.

EVAM EVA YAMANASHI

Threads of stillness run through this hidden cafe, gallery and retail space

~1 hr 40 min

26 min

~10 min

GETTING THERE

From Shinjuku Station, take the JR Chuo Line Limited Express to Kofu Station (~1 hr 40 min). From there take the local train to Higashi-Hanawa (26 min), then a take taxi or local bus to the evam eva complex (~10 min).

evameva-yamanashi.jp

DISCOVER

The store's showroom, gallery and cafe and the surrounding mountains.

SEASONAL HIGHLIGHTS

Spring: plum blossoms. Summer: fruit harvests. Autumn: maples. Winter: snow-tipped serenity.

Advice → *Make sure you book the cafe before you go.*

Overnighter → *Consider making this an overnight stay and combining it with Yamanashi and Kofu wineries (see page 178).*

The train hurtles through valleys and past mountains, but as you approach **Yamanashi**, the pace mellows and those wide skies greet you with wispy cloud-like arms. This is wine, peach and mountain country – and tucked in the region's gentle folds, **evam eva yamanashi**, a destination clothing, restaurant and ceramics space, harnesses all that is good about the surrounding countryside. It's less like a store and more like a meditation. Stepping into evam eva yamanashi, you'll immediately sense the presence of peace.

The clothing is of exceptional quality – minimalist fashion in earthy tones. The mystical Yamanashi light falls gently across racks of linen, wool and cashmere draped like whispers, clothing the colour of fog, stone, sand and rain. Touching the fabric feels like you are touching the seasons. It's a place where you can find that piece that you'll cherish. Because what evam eva gives you is not only clothing, but also a way of moving through the world, a reminder that real luxury is not excess but delicate and still.

Head to the cafe, set in a room with an airy, warm, minimal aesthetic. For lunch, seasonal vegetables are arranged like brushstrokes on ceramics moulded from the very earth that surrounds you. Menus are built around local Yamanashi produce, including vegetables, herbs and regional specialties. Expect set lunches, house-made desserts and beautifully brewed tea and coffee.

Evam eva yamanashi's gallery space features rotating exhibitions of craft, art and design – mostly shining a spotlight on Japanese artisans (quite often local) who work with natural materials. Peruse the covetable homewares, pottery, textiles, handcrafted objects and stationery, ready to select that special piece.

Outside, the garden is a peaceful sculpted landscape that reflects the brand's focus on tranquillity and nature. Somewhere, water trickles. The air smells of cedar and fresh earth. Strolling here instils you with a deep sense of ease, completing your day of inspirational calm.

Evening comes softly. As you catch the train back towards Tokyo, the mountains turn into vast shadows, silhouetted against a darkening sky, and you'll carry that stillness with you, like a thread stitched invisibly into the very fabric of your experience.

WINERIES IN YAMANASHI & KOFU

Fantastic wineries and memorable onsen under Mount Fuji's gaze

Train	~90 min
Train	15–20 min

GETTING THERE

From Shinjuku Station, take the JR Chuo Line Limited Express to Yamanashi Station (~90 min). For Grace Wine and for Hottarakashi Onsen, take the main exit, then take a taxi: it's a 10-minute ride to either destination. For Sadoya Winery, take the Chuo Line to Kofu Station (15–20 min). Take the north exit, then walk 2 minutes to the winery.

yamanashi.kankou.jp

DISCOVER

Grace Wine, Sadoya Winery, Hottarakashi Onsen.

SEASONAL HIGHLIGHTS

Spring: vine blossoms, mountain mists. Summer: flourishing vineyards, clear skies. Autumn: harvest festivals, golden leaves. Winter: sharp Fuji views.

Advice → *Book winery tastings ahead of time. If you've had a few too many and have hired a car, don't drive; Japan has a near-zero blood alcohol limit (0.03 per cent). If you're going to the onsen, pack your onsen kit!*

Overnighter → *Stay the night to make the most of the onsen and visit evam eva yamanashi* *(see page 176)* *the next day.*

Ninety minutes out of Tokyo, the train slows and seems to sigh as it glides into Yamanashi Station and, suddenly, everything breathes differently. The air is clearer, touched by pine and promise. Around you, mountains rise like a sleeping dragon's spine, clouds hanging low and lazy in the brightest blue skies. **Yamanashi** is a cradle of sunlight, hot springs and grapevines that have wrapped themselves around the region for over a thousand years.

Here, wine isn't just poured – it's praised. The translucent Koshu grape, pale and delicate as morning mist, has been cultivated in this soil since long before the word 'vintage' ever found its way to Japan. From Yamanashi Station, it's a 10-minute taxi ride south to **Grace Wine**, where vines stand in quiet formation under the vast Yamanashi sky. Tastings here are sacred little rituals – crisp whites with hints of pears and mountain air; reds that speak in low, smoky tones of volcanic soil. It's intimate, almost reverent – they mean it when they say, 'We do not accept groups of more than four people' – this is a meditation.

Take the Chuo Line to Kofu Station to get to **Sadoya Winery**, a couple of minutes walk away from the station. Founded in 1917, it tells a different story – one of legacy and warmth. Its vaulted cellars and artful pairings feel like stepping into a sepia photograph where the wines are luminous, local and alive with Yamanashi's generous sunlight. Other recommended wineries in the area include **Katsunuma** and **Chateau Sakaori**.

By afternoon, you might be a little light-headed and waxing lyrical about the wonders of the Yamanashi countryside. Time, then, to swap the vineyard breeze for the steam of **Hottarakashi Onsen**, high above the Kofu Basin. Jump on the Chuo Line for the 15–20-minute journey back to Yamanashi Station, then take a taxi ride to the onsen. The name means 'left as it is', and it fits – rustic wooden baths, soft mountain winds, the vast sky unspooling into sunset. Sink into the outdoor pools as Mount Fuji peeks through a cloud veil, pink and bashful.

Stay the night if you can. Dawn here isn't a beginning; it's a revelation – the sun breaking over Fuji's shoulders, the valley glittering below. Yamanashi is known for summer fruits, sweet grapes and peaches so ripe that the juice runs down your chin, so stock up. The vending machines sell bottles of local juice. Pack one in your bag, grab a station bento and carry Yamanashi back to Tokyo with you.

THE STEAMING VALLEY OF JIGOKUDANI

Hot springs with monkeys

90 min

56+ min

9 min

OR

40 min

GETTING THERE

From Tokyo Station, take the Hokuriku Shinkansen to Nagano Station (90 min), then transfer to the Nagaden Railway for Yudanaka Station (catch the Snow Monkey Express if it's running) (56+ min). Take a taxi (9 min) or a bus (40 min) to the Kanbayashi Onsen trailhead.

jigokudani-yaenkoen.co.jp

DISCOVER

Snow Monkey Park, Yudanaka Onsen, Jigokudani Valley.

SEASONAL HIGHLIGHTS

Summer: green forest. Autumn: scarlet foliage framing the valley. Winter: prime monkey-soaking season, magical snow.

Advice → *Wear hiking boots in winter and arrive early before the crowds. Also, this is the land of apples, so make sure you try one.*

Overnighter → *Extend your day trip and visit Shibu Onsen (see page 182) the next day.*

Leave Tokyo in the blue hush of early morning and watch the city unravel behind you as the train speeds towards **Nagano**. Ninety minutes later, the neon fades and the Alps rise like a great white wall. The **Snow Monkey Express** carries you deeper still, into **Yamanouchi** – a land of pine-scented air, old bathhouses and winter roofs quilted in snow. By the time you reach Yudanaka Station, steam curls from sidewalk grates, mom-and-pop shops stack firewood by their doors and everything will feel deliciously slower, softened, hushed.

This valley was once called **Jigokudani (Hell Valley)** – vents hiss steam from the earth and sulphur rises like lost spirits, the whole landscape wreathed in pale white plumes. Yet in this ghostly furnace lies one of Japan's gentlest (and cutest) scenes: wild Japanese macaques soaking in hot springs, faces pinched in bliss, pink cheeks glowing against the winter snow.

From Yudanaka Station, a short bus or taxi ride brings you to the **Kanbayashi Onsen** trailhead. Step into the forest for the 30-minute walk, a pilgrimage through whispering cedars. In summer, it's moss and shade. In winter, the path becomes a monochrome dream – snow creaking underfoot, branches heavy, breath blooming in the frigid air.

Japan's famous troop of wild macaques descend daily from the forest to bathe in the natural hot springs that bubble beside the **Yokoyu River**. The monkeys have been coming here since the 1960s, when local innkeepers first noticed them stealing warmth from outdoor baths. Instead of chasing them off, the villagers built a pool just for them. The entrance to **Snow Monkey Park** feels almost mythical. A small museum honours the generations of 'boss monkeys', their stern portraits watching over the springs like shaggy emperors. And then you'll see the hot springs bath itself: macaques slipping into the water or perched on the edge enjoying the warmth of the steam. Some sit shoulder-deep, eyes half-closed, almost meditating. Mothers cradle tiny babies in the mist. Others methodically groom their companions, the patience almost monastic. It's part wilderness, part family bath-time – an ancient mountain ritual that is both moving and, undeniably, adorable.

Afterwards, wander into the onsen town of **Yudanaka** and warm yourself with a bowl of soba or try a local apple or two, while lantern-lit streets curve around inns and steaming alleys. Here, humans and monkeys both surrender to the mountain's gifts: heat, stillness and the deep beauty of winter.

SHIBU ONSEN

An ancient, steaming onsen town lit by lanterns

Shinkansen		90 min
Train		56+ min
Taxi		5 min
OR Walk		30 min

GETTING THERE

From Tokyo Station, take the Hokuriku Shinkansen to Nagano Station (90 min), then transfer to the Nagaden Railway for Yudanaka Station (catch the Snow Monkey Express if it's running) (56+ min). Take a taxi (5 min) or walk (30 min) to Shibu Onsen.

shibuonsen.net

DISCOVER

Nine public baths, Kawahara-yu (No. 9), Shibu streets at night, Shibu Onsen Temple, local sake bars.

SEASONAL HIGHLIGHTS

Spring: misty mornings, blossoms. Summer: cool mountain evenings. Autumn: colourful foliage framing the alleys. Winter: pure magic – snow, steam, peak onsen vibes.

Overnighter → *If you stay overnight, you get access to all nine baths, so get your onsen kit together! Combine your trip with a visit to Snow Monkey Park (see page 180) to make the most of your time in the region.*

Shibu is the kind of place that seems to exist in myth. Stone alleys wind between wooden inns, and small buildings of warm, dark wood pop into view around each corner. When you arrive, you'll instantly feel the shift – Tokyo's velocity replaced by the soft murmur of unseen streams running beneath the cobbles and gentle mutterings of sulphur, cedar and nostalgia.

Lanterns swing in narrow lanes, lighting the way to the **nine historic bathhouses** that have soothed travellers since the 1300s. Ryokan guests shuffle between them with small towels and wooden keys, drifting from door to door in pursuit of deeper warmth. It feels like stepping inside an old painting – muted colours, drifting steam, silhouettes gliding through mist.

We recommend staying the night. A Shibu inn is a treasure box: centuries-old beams, tatami that smell of sweet straw, shoji screens glowing like paper moons. Dinner arrives in a slow parade – mountain vegetables glazed like jade, amago trout grilled over charcoal, pickled plums sharp on the tongue, delicate miso.

Shibu Onsen feels suspended in time. Samurai once came here to heal; poets to think; the weary to dissolve into mineral spring water. Even now, the streets remain free of neon – only lanterns, geta sandals tapping on stone and the quiet promise of a hot bath waiting around each corner.

Local lore says that bathing in all nine springs brings good fortune; instead, follow the steam to **Bath No. 9, Kawahara-yu**, the oldest and hottest. The heat from its milky waters seep into joints and memory alike.

If you do stay overnight, take one last walk before bed. The temple bell will have fallen silent. The ground radiates heat from hidden pipes. In that quiet moment, you'll feel Shibu's ancient rhythm – water, stone, steam, time – and understand the unbroken thread that links everything in the valley.

THE NAKASENDO: MAGOME TO TSUMAGO

Cedar, stone and memory on the old postal road

Between the mountains of Gifu and Nagano, you'll step into an older Japan – the **Nakasendo**, the slow-beating heart of the Kiso Valley. Here, the 8-kilometre (5-mile) walk from **Magome** to **Tsumago** feels less like a hike and more like travelling through time to find the rhythm of Edo travellers who walked this way long before you.

Morning begins in Magome (43rd post town), perched on its mountainside like a dream. Climb the cobbled slope, past inns built from the darkest, time-polished wood. Waterwheels turn in their own unhurried language; chestnuts roast somewhere out of sight; miso perfumes the air. Buy gohei-mochi lacquered with sweet walnut sauce and eat it still warm, watching clouds stretch and yawn over the mountains. From the **Magome Jinbakami Observatory**, the roofs spread below you in a puzzle of triangles, every one holding its own story. Koi drift in the river, persimmons dry from eaves like plump orange lanterns – autumn announcing itself in fruit.

Late morning will carry you into the forest, the stones softening into earth, the light shifting into long, green breaths. This part of the Nakasendo is gentle – 2.5 to 3 hours at an easy pace, mostly downhill. Woodsmoke curls between farmhouses; bamboo leans in close; the air tastes of pine. Bear bells hang on posts like tiny guardians. **Kumanojinja Shrine** is vibrant, especially in autumn. Mist floats between the cedars. At **Ichikokutochi Tateba Chaya** you'll find a small thatched teahouse and visitor centre where volunteers may welcome you with cups of green tea and warm smiles. There's no charge, though donations are accepted – the Edo tradition of roadside hospitality very much alive. Sit for a moment, admiring the double-flowered weeping cherry before you and letting the warmth of the tea move through your hands and into your body, reviving tired limbs. Further along you'll encounter the **Odaki** and **Medaki waterfalls**, scenic cascades of water that are considered male and female and were once used in purification rituals.

- ~90 min
- 50–60 min
- 25 min

GETTING THERE

From Tokyo Station, take the Tokaido Shinkansen to Nagoya Station (~90 min), then transfer to the Shinano Limited Express to Nakatsugawa Station (50–60 min). From the main exit, a local bus winds through the hills to Magome (25 min), where the trail begins.

kiso-nagano.or.jp

DISCOVER

Magome waterwheels; Kumanojinja Shrine; Ichikokutochi Tateba Chaya; Odaki and Medaki waterfalls; Waki-Honjin Okuya; Tsumago's preserved streets.

SEASONAL HIGHLIGHTS

Spring: cherry blossoms, soft mist. Summer: bright greens, warm streams. Autumn: peak colours, crisp air – the best walking season. Winter: quiet, snow-powdered, magical but icy on slopes.

Advice → *Walk from Magome to Tsumago as it is easier going downhill. From Tsumago, you can take a 7-minute bus or taxi to Nagiso Station, or walk about 20 minutes along quiet roads. From Nagiso Station, trains connect easily back to Nagoya, and onwards to Tokyo. Wear good walking shoes, bring water and carry cash for snacks and small donations.*

Weekender → *Both towns offer minshuku, often historic family-run inns, or kominka, old farmhouses renovated and turned into inns, as accommodation options.*

This is a great resource: https://en.nagiso.jp/topics_category/stay/

After some more of the splendid scenery, begin your descent into **Tsumago**. The forest will eventually open to reveal one of Japan's best-preserved post towns, lining the **Araragi River**. Wooden inns with latticed windows look over paper lanterns swaying gently on the narrow street. Electric wires are hidden here, and cars are few – preserving the Edo atmosphere. The **Waki-Honjin Okuya**, once an inn for high-ranking officials, is now a museum where light filters through paper shoji onto tatami mats and polished beams, conjuring the same golden hush that once greeted weary travellers. Views can be enjoyed from the **Tsumago Castle Ruins** at the fork of the **Kiso River**. Browse small craft and omiyage shops, famous for Kiso Valley hinoki products – chopsticks, trays and rice-warming buckets that smell faintly of cypress.

When we did this walk, we finished with a simple meal of soba noodles, oyaki dumplings and seasonal mountain vegetables, along with a well-earned sake, celebrating the fortitude of our legs and a newly found resilience in our spirits.

Churches of stone, wood and light in the first Western resort in Japan

~70 min

GETTING THERE

From Tokyo Station, take the Hokuriku Shinkansen to Karuizawa Station (~70 min). Take the north exit. Local trains connect to Naka-Karuizawa.

karuizawa-kankokyokai.jp

DISCOVER

Mampei Hotel, Former Mikasa Hotel, St Paul's Catholic Church, Shaw Memorial Church, Hoshino Kogen Church, Hoshino Stone Church, Karuizawa Taliesin, Old Karuizawa villas, Hoshino Hotel.

SEASONAL HIGHLIGHTS

Spring: blooms, bright forest light. Autumn: colourful foliage, peak season.

Advice → *Churches observe quiet rules; no photographs inside the churches. Book ahead to eat at Mampei Hotel. Explore by rental bicycle. Wear good walking shoes and bring layers – mountain weather can shift fast. The gorgeous Hoshino Hotel offers day onsen bathing at their other-worldly Tombo-no-Yu bathhouse.*

Overnighter → *Save up like we did and spend the night at the Mampei Hotel.*

Karuizawa is unlike other day trips in this book – a fusion of nature, spirit and architecture shaped by wandering missionaries, Western dreamers and the patience of the Nakasendo Road. Once a quiet post town, Karuizawa was transformed in 1886 after Anglican minister Alexander Croft Shaw arrived; he imagined a sanctuary of lodges, spired chapels and modernist visions rising among the pines, thus creating Japan's first true Western-style mountain retreat.

Morning rises gently at the historic **Mampei Hotel**. John and Yoko loved it here, and as you sit in the wood-panelled cafe beneath portraits of diplomats and artists, you'll understand why. Warm wood, shoji screens, Western armchairs, polished boards – East and West in quiet dialogue. Anyone can visit for breakfast or tea, even without staying, though the temptation to linger is strong. Further into the town, past towering cypress, the **Former Mikasa Hotel** – Japan's first all-Western hotel – stands like an elegant time capsule, a notable counterpoint to the traditional ryokan. You can walk there from town; it's a bit of a hike but we recommend it because the abundant forested residential architecture you'll see along the way is fascinating: Western mid-century homes, log cabins and minimal museum-like architectural details in luxury abodes. None of it resembles the Japan you know. The Mikasa itself is a grand, many-roomed lodge with a flamboyant, ornate, latticed frontage that must have been (and remains) a visually impressive first impression.

This town is popular with couples young and old. Wander the leafy lanes near Karuizawa Station, where the town's spiritual beginnings hide among the trees. **St Paul's Catholic Church**, designed by Antonin Raymond, looks simple from the outside – a peaked, almost barn-like shape – but inside, its vaulted wooden ceiling astounds. Nearby, the humble **Shaw Memorial Church**, built in 1885, still echoes the same promise that first drew Shaw here: a place where faith and forest are one.

From there, head to the **Hoshino Hotel** enclave, a short stroll from Naka-Karuizawa Station. The **Hoshino Kogen Church**, Karuizawa's most famous, rises like a glass-and-wood triangle lifted by light itself – a chapel that changes with the seasons, its roof catching petals in spring and red leaves in autumn. A short walk away, the **Hoshino Stone Church** astonishes with its undulating arcs of stone and glass, Kendrick Kellogg's retro-futurist meditation on gravity, moss and water. He was a protégé of Frank Lloyd Wright, whose influence is apparent, but Kellogg clearly had a determination to pave his own way. The church and the small subterranean chapel feel alive, like something the forest dreamt into being.

As the long day closes, stroll through **Old Karuizawa**, past mid-century villas hidden behind mossed walls, cedar frames glowing in the late light. By day, visitors flock here, enjoying perfect soba noodles at popular places like **Kawakamian**, or visiting the past in atmospheric kissaten **Café L'Opera**. The **Karuizawa New Art Museum** and the **Wakita Museum of Art** put a surprising, contemporary spin on the area. Near Mampei, the cobbled **'Happy Valley' trail** is girded by greenery and low stone walls. The air smells of fern, bark and cedar and a freshness that can only come with the country. In every eave and beam, the old promise remains: a mountain refuge built on stillness, creativity and reverence.

Karuizawa Nature Walk

Enjoy rambling through Karuizawa's wooded heart – footsteps muffled by moss; the air fresh and alive; paths fringed with hedges, white birch, oak and maple. These two routes link three of the area's most peaceful sites – the **Yacho no Mori (Karuizawa Wild Bird Sanctuary)**, **Kumoba Pond** and **Shiraito Falls**. You can tackle it as one large day trip or stay overnight and split it into two.

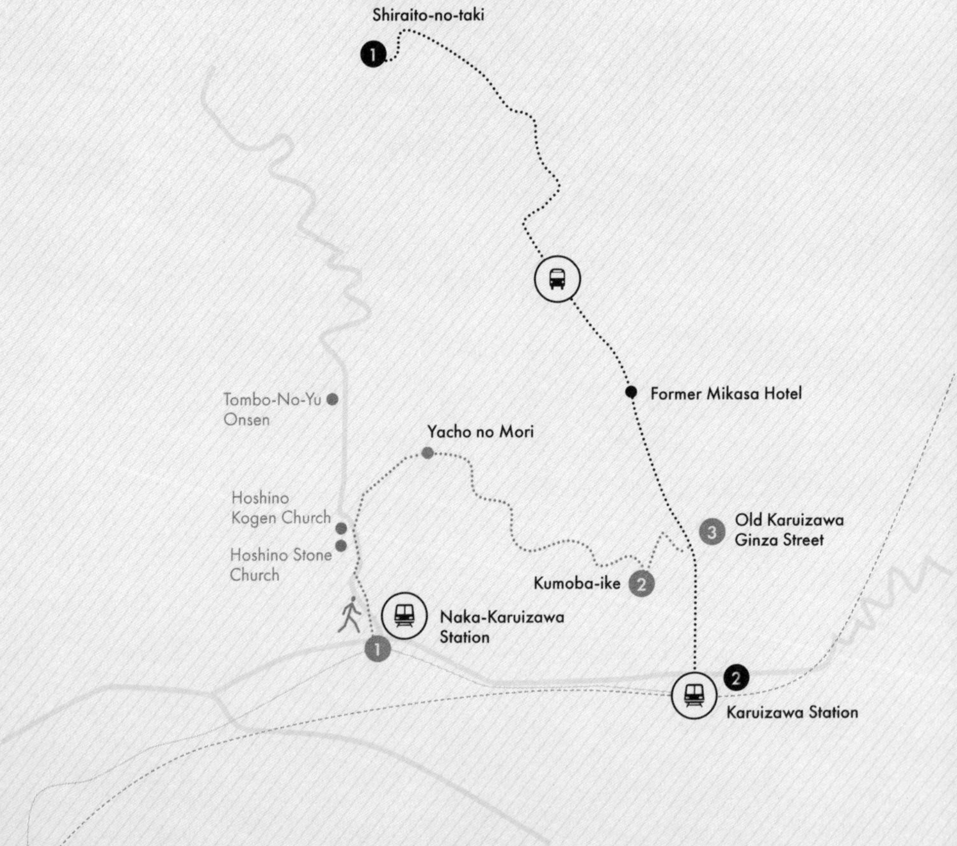

PATH 1 Duration: 4–5 hours, depending on pace | Difficulty: Easy, with a mix of urban streets and gentle hills

PATH 2 Duration: 2+ hours, depending on pace | Difficulty: Easy

PATH 1

1 START AT NAKA-KARUIZAWA STATION

Rent a bicycle or walk to the **Yacho no Mori (Karuizawa Wild Bird Sanctuary)**, a 100-hectare (247-acre) protected forest where the beauty of avian life plays out among the treetops.

The trail winds below tall red pines and birch, where woodpeckers and flycatchers flash between the trunks. Benches along the way invite quiet meditation and observation.

Distance: 2.8 kilometres (1.7 miles)

2 RIDE OR WALK TO KUMOBA-IKE

Nicknamed the 'Swan Lake of Karuizawa', **Kumoba-ike (Kumoba Pond)** mirrors the surrounding trees in its perfectly still surface. In autumn, the crimson trees appear both above and within the water. A gentle 20-minute path circles the pond – ideal for a mid-morning stroll.

Distance: 4.4 kilometres (2.7 miles)

3 LUNCH IN OLD KARUIZAWA

Cafes around the **Ginza Street** area serve local vegetables and buckwheat noodles – light, earthy fare for the walk ahead. The road just south of Kumoba Pond, running into Karuizawa's centre, is part of the old Nakasendo Trail, so you can add it to your tally if you're walking other parts of the trail.

PATH 2

1 TRAVEL TO SHIRAITO-NO-TAKI

Take the local bus from Karuizawa Station to **Shiraito-no-taki (Shiraito Falls)** (25 min). A 5-minute forest path leads to a curtain of water cascading like liquid glass through ferns and moss. It will be unlike any waterfall you have seen. Though only 3 metres (10 feet) high, it's an impressive 70 metres (230 feet) wide, giving it the appearance of a wall of thin water ribbons. It lives up to its name, which translates as 'waterfall of white threads'.

Distance: 11 kilometres (6.8 miles)

2 RETURN TO KARUIZAWA STATION

Catch a return bus to the station or stop off at the Former Mikasa Hotel (see page 189), which is on the same bus route.

Distance to Former Mikasa Hotel: 7 kilometres (4.3 miles)

Distance from Former Mikasa Hotel to Karuizawa Station: 4 kilometres (2.5 miles)

KUSATSU ONSEN

Sulphur and steam in an onsen town with a spectacular central water channel

~70 min

~80 min

OR

~2 hr 20 min

25–30 min

GETTING THERE

From Tokyo Station, take the Hokuriku Shinkansen to Karuizawa Station (~70 min), then transfer to the Kusatsu Express bus to Kusatsu Onsen Bus Terminal (~80 min). Or, from Ueno Station, take the JR Limited Express Kusatsu to Naganohara-Kusatsuguchi Station (~2 hr 20 min), then a JR bus to Kusatsu Onsen Bus Terminal (25–30 min).

kusatsu-onsen.ne.jp/guide/en/

DISCOVER

Yubatake, Netsu-no-Yu, Sai-no-Kawara Park and Open-Air Bath, Kosen-ji Temple, shops for manju, hinoki crafts and onsen tamago.

SEASONAL HIGHLIGHTS

Spring: gentle warmth, fresh greenery. Autumn: fiery maples and rising mist. Winter: snow-draped town, steaming baths.

Advice → *Bring a small towel for washing and a larger one for drying. Buses stop running early in the evening, so check return times.*

Kusatsu Onsen will appear before you with drifting plumes of white – a highland town where heat and cold live in a kind of permanent tension. It's a long day trip, but the moment you arrive, the travel will melt away. **Kusatsu** moves to its own pace, a heartbeat powered by the great **Yubatake** – the steaming 'hot water field' at its centre. Water nearly 70°C (158°F) in temperature gushes through a cedar grid, roaring and hissing, cooling as it tumbles towards the town's many baths and pipes that heat schools, buildings and homes. It feels alive, like a benevolent mountain spirit. Steam wafts upwards in soft white columns; the air smells of sulphur and sweet wood.

Around the Yubatake, narrow cobbled lanes curve between ryokan, teahouses and wooden shopfronts. Wander slowly, carrying your onsen kit of towels and toiletries. At **Netsu-no-Yu**, pause for the yumomi ritual: women in patterned yukata rhythmically paddle the steaming waters, singing Edo-era folk songs that echo through the warm haze.

Kusatsu has the largest natural flow of hot spring water in Japan, and its highly acidic springs are famed nationwide for their healing power. With a Choina Pass in hand, you can hop between the town's signature baths – the elegant **Gozano-yu**, the very hot **Ohtakino-yu** and, our favourite, the open-air **Sai-no-Kawara** bath. To reach it, follow Sainokawara Street past omiyage stores; onsen manju vendors; shops selling hinoki bath bowls, onsen towels and yukata; and steaming egg baskets where onsen tamago cook in the bubbling springs. The half-hour walk into the park will lead you past vents exhaling steam slowly from the earth. Inside, the bath is a vast, milky-blue pool beneath murmuring pines. The water here, drawn from the same volcanic source as the Yubatake, is said to heal everything but heartbreak, although we think it would go a long way to cheering anyone lamenting lost love.

Later, warm yourself with soba, onigiri or a sweet red-bean manju. In winter, maitake mushroom tempura soba feels like a blessing. We chose to stay overnight to climb the short trail to **Kosen-ji Temple**, which overlooks the Yubatake. The view at dusk is unforgettable – the whole town dressed in steam, lanterns amber through the haze, the Yubatake glowing below. When we left, the bus descended into night. The sulphur faded. And in our heads, the yumomi songs kept time with the road.

HARA MUSEUM ARC

A minimalist dialogue between modern art and the countryside

~50 min

~20 min

15 min

OR

25 min

GETTING THERE

From Tokyo Station, take the Joetsu Shinkansen to Takasaki Station (~50 min), then transfer to the JR Joetsu Line for Shibukawa Station (~20 min). From Shibukawa Station's west exit, take a taxi (15 min) or bus (25 min) towards Ikaho Onsen and hop off at Green Bokujo-mae, then it's a short walk to the museum.

haramuseum.or.jp

DISCOVER

Kankai Pavilion (ARC Pavilion), Warhol's giant sculpture *Campbell's Tomato Soup*, Yayoi Kusama's *Mirror Room (Pumpkin)*, Yoshitomo Nara's *My Drawing Room*.

SEASONAL HIGHLIGHTS

Spring and autumn: surrounding mountains frame mirrored pavilions in soft green and burnished gold.

Advice → *Please note, the museum is shut from January to March.*

Overnighter → *Enjoy an overnight stay in Gunma's fertile uplands by combining this day trip with Ikaho Onsen (see page 198), Mizusawa Udon Street and Haruna Shrine.*

Most museums in the city hum with life, the sound of crowds filling the halls. The **Hara Museum ARC**, nestled in the highlands near **Ikaho Onsen**, is quiet and contemplative. It inhabits, and is inhabited by, the landscape. Designed by Arata Isozaki and opened in 1988, the museum is splayed out in a field like a wooden insect with open wings. Wooden huts and barns are so dark that surface details are completely lost, and yet the spaces themselves are stark shapes against the bright grass. Its dark wood walls reflect the shifting weather: morning mist clings to windows and afternoon clouds are drifting reflections in panels of glass. When you walk the grounds, you enter a gentle conversation between architecture, air and art.

Inside, white corridors unfold into intimate galleries. Works from the **Hara Museum Collection** – minimalist sculptures, contemporary Japanese installations and international modern art – are deliberately spaced out, a decision that gives each piece its own focus. The collection itself reflects a century of contemplation: Warhol and Richter beside Japanese avant-garde, all highlighted by filtered daylight that spills through Isozaki's architectural arcs.

We found we had many favourite exhibits among the works. Warhol's large outdoor *Campbell's Tomato Soup* can seem out of place yet also perfectly placed in its exterior home in the elements. Jean-Michel Othoniel's *Kokoro* provides an excellent opportunity for photographs, the emotive upright heart framing the gallery building. Inside, Yayoi Kusama's *Mirror Room (Pumpkin)* may be a familiar theme, but this is one of her best – a yellow infinity room where pumpkins and dots, replicated into infinity, surround and engulf you. Yoshitomo Nara's *My Drawing Room*, transplanted from Tokyo's now sadly defunct Hara Museum, is one of a series of artworks that whimsically replicate the artist's actual workspace, so that viewers can be closer to his process or perhaps become voyeurs of his creations.

The Hara Museum ARC is not large, but it makes an impression. We love to travel for art, and this place of calm in Gunma's rarified air is the perfect example of how the remoteness of a gallery is not a barrier but the very reason to go.

IKAHO ONSEN

Stone steps, lanterns and drifting steam

- ~50 min
- ~20 min
- 15+ min

GETTING THERE

From Tokyo Station, take the Joetsu Shinkansen to Takasaki Station (~50 min), then transfer to the JR Joetsu Line for Shibukawa Station (~20 min). From Shibukawa Station's west exit, take a bus (25 min) or a taxi (15 min) or to Ikaho Onsen.

visit-gunma.jp

DISCOVER

Ikaho Stone Steps (lined with inns, cafes and old bathhouses), Ikaho Shrine, rotenburo (outdoor bath) with views over the mountains, Kajika Bridge, Ikaho Ropeway for vistas of Mount Haruna and the valley below.

SEASONAL HIGHLIGHTS

Spring: plum blossoms, gentle mountain mist. Autumn: leaves glowing through onsen steam. Winter: snow-dusted steps, golden baths.

Advice → *If the stone steps feel like too much, take the ropeway up to Tokimeki Deck for a memorable view of Ikaho Onsen and the surrounding countryside.*

Overnighter → *Combine this day trip with nearby Hara Museum ARC (see page 196) and enjoy a perfect overnight stay.*

It may not be for the faint-hearted, but the stone steps, 365 in all, that lead to the heart of **Ikaho Onsen** feel both like an ascent through the centuries and a walk into the heart of relaxation. Twelve inns lean closely over the stairway to Heaven (others wait quietly down alleyways), each marked by a zodiac sign on the stone walkway, each with wooden facades darkened by time and steam. The rhythm of the climb is marked by sound: the slow shuffle of geta sandals, a shopkeeper calling out from a window, the sound of laughter from holiday-makers in summer yukata. Many footbaths also appear as a blessing while you climb, so take time to soak those tired feet!

One of Japan's oldest hot spring towns, **Ikaho** has a popular hot springs bath – **Ikaho Rotenburo** (outdoor bath) – where a rusty golden spring, rich with iron, runs amber through the pipes and leaves its mark, staining wooden baths with warm ochre hues. Rising from a volcanic source deep beneath **Mount Haruna**, the waters flow as they have for a thousand years, a potent blending of history and relaxation. Nearby, vermillion **Kajika Bridge** is resplendent, especially in autumn foliage.

The **Ikaho Shrine**, midway up the steps, offers respite from the climb as well as a spectacular view. From its wooden verandah, the town below appears spread out – steam floating up in small white ribbons against a backdrop of verdant mountains. Enjoy the view before taking in the nearby rotenburo onsen waters.

On the (much easier) way down, stop for a bowl of cold Mizusawa udon, Gunma's specialty and known as one of Japan's three great udon noodles. Another delectable treat in Ikaho Onsen is an onsen manju, a bun cooked by the mineral steam. Now popular across Japan, they were first invented here, so take the time to partake. If time and energy permit, ascend Mount Haruna on the **Ikaho Ropeway** for some memorable views of the surrounding terrain.

As the light fades, Ikaho glows. Steam curls through the alleys, catching the lantern light, and people in ryokan head to their evening baths. Somewhere deep beneath the ground, the golden spring keeps running – an eternal current, whispering of a deep, relaxing pause set among the flow of time.

KUBOTA ITCHIKU ART MUSEUM

Meditative, reverent, luminous – an homage to beauty and patience

Train	~70 min
Train	~55 min
Bus / Taxi	15 min

GETTING THERE

From Shinjuku Station, take the Chuo Line Limited Express to Otsuki Station (~70 min), then transfer to the Fujikyu Railway for Kawaguchiko Station (~55 min). From Kawaguchiko Station's main exit, a 15-minute bus or taxi ride goes directly to the museum.

thekubotacollection.com

DISCOVER

Spectacular kimono textile art, Lake Kawaguchi, Mount Fuji views.

SEASONAL HIGHLIGHTS

Autumn: maples frame the Lake Kawaguchi Maple Corridor.

Advice → *Although Fuji can be seen from the museum's cafe on a clear day, head to the nearby shores of Lake Kawaguchi for panoramic Fuji views.*

Overnighter → *Spend the night at Lake Kawaguchi (see page 202) to enjoy those Fuji views in the morning. In autumn, stroll through the Lake Kawaguchi Maple Corridor displays bright colours just minutes from the lake's edge.*

At the foot of Mount Fuji, where the mountain preens in the mirror surface of **Lake Kawaguchi**, there stands a unique museum, made not of marble, steel or glass but of coral, limestone and timber – the **Kubota Itchiku Art Museum**. It is a reverent sanctuary for Kubota's kimono art, a sanctum of light where dyed cloth reflects sky, sea and eternity.

Itchiku Kubota revived a lost dyeing technique called tsujigahana, practised in the 16th century. After decades of study and experimentation, Kubota created his own version, Itchiku tsujigahana, using silk, ink, precision and patience. Other-worldly, mystical yet familiar landscapes are painted onto large kimono, hung suspended in the air or against walls, coming alive when touched by light.

The museum was designed by Kubota, the site purposefully chosen for both its proximity to Mount Fuji and its forested surrounds. Kubota was inspired by the great mountain and this can be seen in his *Fuji* series, which is on display in the gallery. The museum's thatched roofs and stone walls echo traditional mountain dwellings and seem at one with the surrounding greenery. Water trickles down mossed steps, and walls undulate and curve, organic shapes with a Spanish flavour that recalls Gaudi's living architecture. Inside, light is filtered through handmade glass, falling softly on the rows of striking kimono.

The centrepiece is *Symphony of Light*, a series depicting the universe and the shifting seasons – a continuous panorama that was intended to include 80 pieces, although only 30 were completed before Kubota's death. Robes are covered in scattered autumn leaves, gently rising waves or night skies deep with indigo and gold. Standing before them, you forget the medium – silk and dye become living worlds on the kimono canvas. The folds of each kimono hold the story of decades spent conjuring colour from time.

Outside, the **museum gardens** frame a view of Mount Fuji, sometimes veiled in mist, sometimes staggeringly sharp. Small sculptures line pathways, and a teahouse serves matcha overlooking the pond – a fitting stillness after the urgency of the colour within.

The Kubota museum is not a large space, yet it plays host to worlds. It is a museum about devotion – to art, to creation and to the sacred rhythm of making. In this temple of colour, cloth is no longer fashion or form; it is an act of prayer.

LAKE KAWAGUCHI

Fuji, the lake and the sky

~70 min

~55 min

GETTING THERE

From Shinjuku Station, take the Chuo Line Limited Express to Otsuki Station (~70 min), then transfer to the Fujikyu Railway for Kawaguchiko Station (~55 min). From Kawaguchiko Station's main exit, local buses, taxis or rental bikes connect all major viewpoints around the lake.

japan.travel/en/spot/1329

DISCOVER

Mount Fuji Panoramic Ropeway, Lake Kawaguchi north shore, Oishi Park.

SEASONAL HIGHLIGHTS

Spring: cherry blossoms, snow-topped Fuji mirrored in the lake. Autumn: maples, glassy still water. Winter: clear skies for the most vivid Fuji views.

Advice → *Other excellent things to do in the area include the Music Forest and flower arranging at Herb Hall.*

Overnighter → *Combine this day trip with nearby Kubota Itchiku Art Museum (see page 200), and stay overnight to make the most of it all.*

Leaving Kawaguchiko Station, the air feels new – thinner, cooler, carrying the scent of pine and mountain ash. The town of **Kawaguchiko** itself is small and peaceful, and has long been one of the premier spots to witness Mount Fuji in all its majesty. We always feel that to walk along the northern shore of **Lake Kawaguchi** and see Fuji mirrored perfectly in the water is to live in a metaphor – reflecting upon one of the world's great reflections. For us, early morning is the best time: the stillness of the lake is a highly polished mirror and the mountain is a vision, suspended in blue. So we recommend staying over and making a mini-break of it. However, it also works perfectly as a day trip from Tokyo.

For one of the great lake views, head to **Oishi Park**, where paths wend their way through flowerbeds that change with the seasons: tulips in spring, lavender in summer, cosmos and vibrant maples in autumn. Across the lake, Fuji looms, the colourful floral displays a fitting tribute. Cafes serve lavender ice cream and offer places where you can relax and watch the mountain drift in and out of cloud.

From here, take a short taxi ride to the **Mount Fuji Panoramic Ropeway**, which ascends to **Tenjoyama Park**, where you can get a scenic view of the lake and a peacocking Fuji beyond. The expansive view is breathtaking, the volcano's slopes leading down to the glinting water, the horizon fenced with cedar. In winter, Fuji tips its cloud hat, dapper in a cloak of snow.

Enjoy a late lunch or early dinner of the local specialty, hoto noodles, thick and warming. As the sun begins to dissolve, return to the lakeshore. The sky blushes violet and rose and Fuji's peak catches the last diamond glint of daylight. Later, the train hums back to Tokyo, and the mountain becomes a lasting memory.

おみやげ　お休処
塚本みやげ店
民芸の店 塚本
おかえりなさいませ
おみやげ
ゑびすや
お休所

A pilgrim's trail to a mountain shrine with a majestic view

Train		49 min
Bus		~25 min
Cable car		5 min

GETTING THERE

From Shinjuku Station, take the Odakyu Line Romancecar to Isehara Station (49 min). From the north exit, take the bus to Oyama Cable Car Station (~25 min).

afuri.or.jp

DISCOVER

Lower and Upper Afuri Shrine, Oyama-mairi pilgrimage path, summit views of Fuji and Enoshima, Otoko-zaka trail, waterfalls, teahouses, Oyama Cable Car.

SEASONAL HIGHLIGHTS

Spring: fresh greens, cool air, full waterfalls. Summer: lush forest. Autumn: brilliant maple colours, misty trails, lively teahouses, peak season. Winter: crisp skies, Fuji views, icy sections on trails.

Advice → *Wear sturdy shoes; the summit path is steep and rocky. Carry water and snacks. Fog is common – check weather for Fuji views. Weekends in autumn will be very busy.*

Isehara Station sits just northwest of the Enoshima–Kamakura coastline, but instead of drifting south towards the sea, turn your feet towards **Mount Oyama** – a sacred peak that has drawn pilgrims upwards for more than a thousand years. From the station, a small bus threads through narrow neighbourhood streets, steepening towards the foothills until you reach Oyama Cable Car Station. This is the threshold, the ancient starting point of the **Oyama-mairi pilgrimage**.

Catch the cable car up to **Afuri Shrine**, or if you are here for the full hike, begin your climb at the base, beneath rustling cedars; wooden way-markers polished by centuries of prayerful touch line the paths. There are two paths available: the women's and the men's. They both take around 35 minutes and end up at the shrine. The air is a blend of pine, earth and the warm soy-sweet perfume of miso oden bubbling in old teahouses. Whenever we've passed by on this walk, the women tending the kettles haved called out, 'Ganbatte!' – do your best – their voices cutting through the mist with the same cheerful encouragement given to pilgrims long before us.

The shrine's vermillion buildings stand poised against deep forest green; its torii frames distant Tokyo like a tiny mirage far below. Pause here to listen to the wind carrying bells and crowsong through the valley, before you push higher. The spectacular upper part of the Afuri Shrine can be reached by a long series of steps, and the walk is almost a hike in itself.

From the left of the shrine, the true hike begins, leading to the top of Mount Oyama. The path steepens dramatically, becoming a lattice of roots and moss-coated stones. Clouds may drift low, mist brushing your shoulders, and you'll likely feel as though the mountain is testing you just a little. After about 2 hours you'll reach the summit, breathless but triumphant. On clear days, Mount Fuji appears – floating, gleaming, perfect – while to the south is a distant Enoshima Island. Even in fog, there is a solemn beauty here, the sense that Oyama keeps its own weather, its own secrets. A full hike from the base can take around 4 to 5 hours, so consider your options.

Back at the shrine, take the opportunity to glide down by cable car (the last one is usually at 5 pm), suspended in drifting mist. Evening pools in the valleys below. Oyama will fade into shadow behind you, yet you will still feel its presence – a quiet guardian watching over the plains.

ADVENTURES IN CHICHIBU

Kannon pilgrimages, shrines, retro streets, onsen and sake

~80 min

GETTING THERE

From Ikebukuro Station, take the Seibu Ikebukuro Line Limited Express Laview to Seibu-Chichibu Station (~80 min). Take the main exit.

chichibu-omotenashi.com

DISCOVER

Chichibu's 34 Kannon temples, Chichibu Shrine carvings, Arakawa River gorges and bridges, Hitsujiyama Park.

SEASONAL HIGHLIGHTS

Spring: moss phlox and Shibazakura Festival at Hitsujiyama Park (early April to early May). Summer: scenic riverside walks, cooler mountain air. Autumn: flaming maples in temple courtyards. Winter: Chichibu Yomatsuri (Night Festival; 2–3 December).

Advice → *Train seats must be reserved. Try Chichibu's famed waraji-katsudon, deep-fried pork cutlets served on rice (their size rivals the straw sandals they're named after). Street stalls sell miso potato skewers and the local sake is also revered, made with the freshest mountain water.*

Weekender → *Turn this day trip into a mini-break and choose from the walks on* *pages 210–215.*

The Chichibu Go 15, Seibu's Limited Express train, travels briskly through hills and vales, carrying you towards a Japan out of time – leisurely, more gentle, fringed by mountains and imbued with history.

Chichibu is a chameleon, morphing with the seasons. In autumn, nature embraces the city. Upstream on the **Arakawa River** you'll find verdant hidden gorges. In **Nagatoro**, boats float languidly between sheer rock cliffs and valleys are afire with deep red maples and golden ginkgo. In winter, illuminated icicle formations create a stunning effect. Yet one could argue that spring is the best time to go, when the town looks like a riot of paint strokes on an artist's canvas. Impressionistic colour swathes the land and the mountainsides are redolent with flowers. Just a short walk from the station you'll find **Hitsujiyama Park**, where the notable **Shibazakura Hill** is dressed in vibrant pink moss phlox from late April to early May. Nearly 400,000 varietal blooms dance across the slopes in waves of magenta, lavender and white – a dream-like sequence of colour and texture.

Chichibu is part of the famous **34 Kannon Pilgrimage**, a hike past some 1300 statues of the Buddha and 34 of the 100 Japanese Kannon temples. You can extend this to a much longer hike if you'd like, but within the central area of Chichibu, you'll find many wonders in the 6–7-kilometre (4-mile) walk from **En'yu-ji Temple** to **Chosen-in Temple**. Narrow streets, mossy stairways, towering trees and abundant foliage accompany you on your trek. There are several one-day trails, one of the most popular being the scenic route from Owa Bus Stop to **Mitsumine Shrine**. This slightly strenuous 4-hour trek takes you to the shrine, atmospheric and tranquil among the trees. For a more breezy stroll, however, you can head to the town centre, where you'll find **Chichibu Shrine**, one of the region's finest. You'll be fascinated by its carved beams and vivid colours – dragons, tigers and phoenixes rippling across the eaves. As you can see, there's a lot to do in Chichibu, so why not turn your day trip into a weekender?

Chichibu streets are fairly quiet on regular days, but the area features some of Japan's best-known festivals and this is when the town truly comes alive. The **Chichibu Yomatsuri (Night Festival)** in December is the best known. Beautifully constructed floats the size of houses glide through lantern-lit streets, soundtracked by taiko drums and the pop and crack of fireworks. Time your visit to join in the festivities, or head to the **Chichibu Festival Museum** to see displays of past festival floats.

武甲正宗
武甲
宝暦三年創業
銘酒
武甲正宗
柳田總本店
キリンビール

秩父
武甲正宗
本醸造
ひさご徳利
秩父
700円

Chichibu is also known as a sake destination. Pick up a Chichibu Sake Map at the tourist information centre outside the station. Our favourite sake brewery is the rustic **Buko Shuzo**, a 10-minute walk south from Seibu-Chichibu Station along Route 140. This beautifully preserved brewery uses pure underground spring water from Mount Buko. You can join a short guided tour (free, ~20 minutes) and sample several types of Buko masamune. The brewery is open from 9 am to 4.30 pm.

A Chichibu Big Day Out

This is an easy day walk with a lovely mix of retro buildings in Chichibu Town, a spectacular shrine, nature and a relaxing soak.

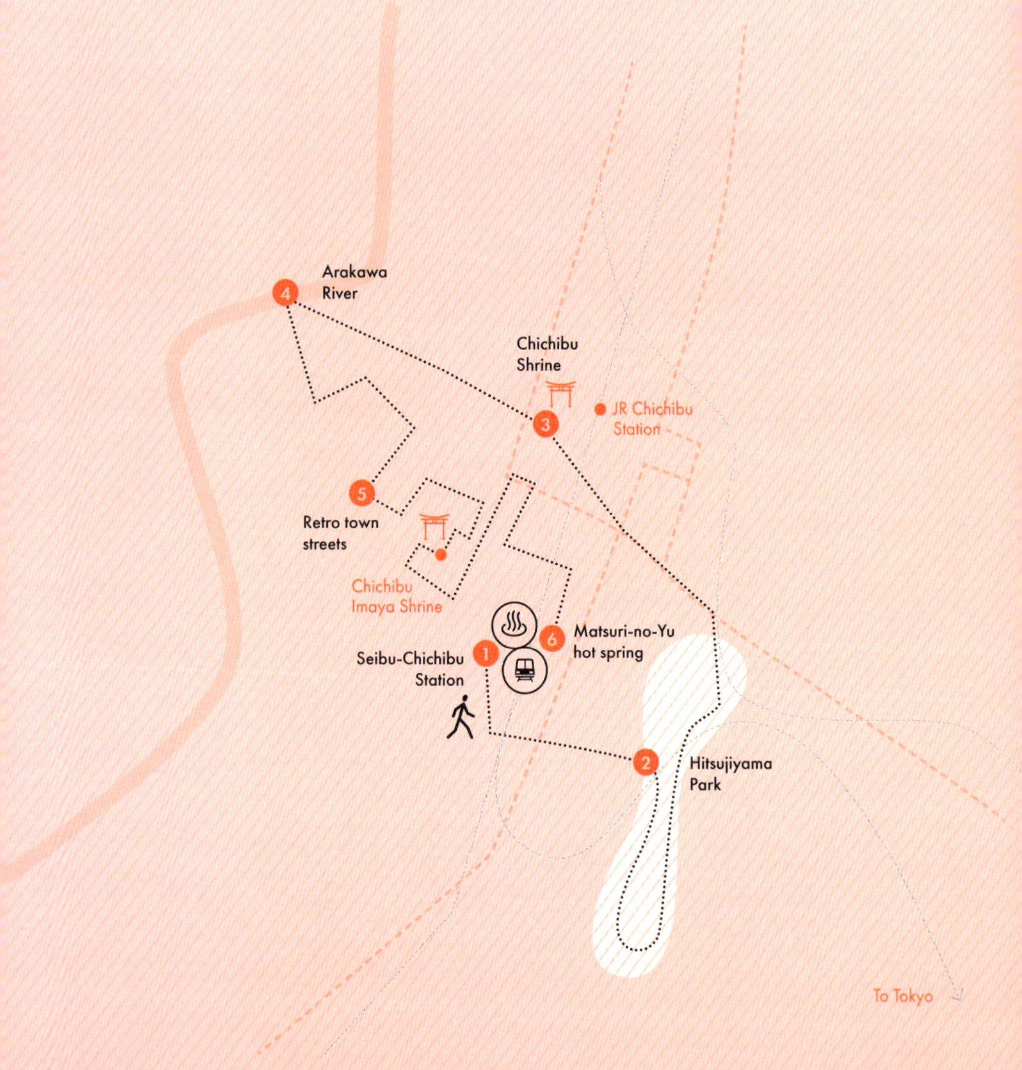

Duration: 3–5 hours, depending on pace | Difficulty: Easy, with a mix of urban streets and gentle hills

1 START AT SEIBU-CHICHIBU STATION

Arrive via the limited express from Ikebukuro Station. Pick up a map at the station or the tourist information centre.

2 HITSUJIYAMA PARK

Make your way towards **Hitsujiyama Park**. In April and May, the park bursts into life with the **Shibazakura Festival**, a carpet of pink moss phlox across rolling fields. Outside flowering season, the park still offers great views across the town to the surrounding mountains.

3 CHICHIBU SHRINE

Begin at the Chichibu Shrine, admiring its brilliantly painted carvings – dragons, tigers and phoenixes.

4 ARAKAWA RIVER WALK

Cross the Arakawa River towards the **Takenohana Bridge** for sweeping views of the basin and Mount Buko. Pause by the water's edge – the emerald river is swift and refreshing.

5 RETRO TOWN STREETS

Wander towards the shopping streets near the shrine. Browse family-run shops selling handmade miso, wagashi and local sake. Try waraji-katsudon, the famous oversized pork cutlet, for a hearty lunch.

6 MATSURI-NO-YU HOT SPRING

Circle back to Seibu-Chichibu Station. Before boarding the train, stop at the station's **Matsuri-no-Yu hot spring** for a relaxing soak or foot bath. The station also has an amazing array of food options.

Advice → Visit in spring for blossoms or in autumn for foliage.

Mitsumine Shrine Day Walk

A hike with glorious views. We recommend starting early and moving at your own pace. Make sure to send out a cheery 'konnichiwa' to fellow hikers.

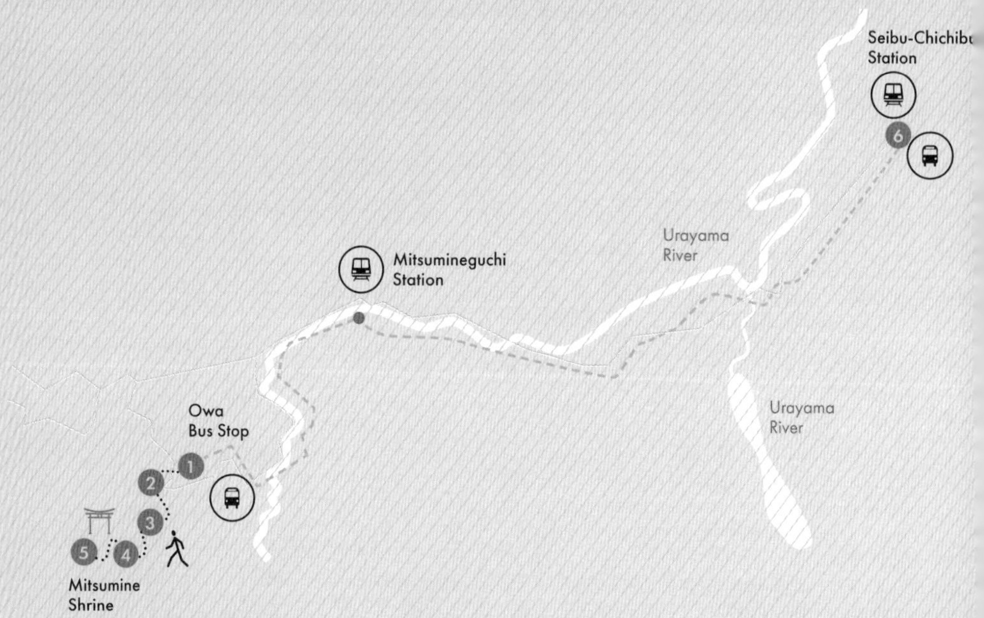

Duration: 3–5 hours, depending on pace | Difficulty: Moderate

At Seibu-Chichibu Station, transfer to a Seibu Kanko or Chichibu bus bound for Mitsumine Shrine and get off at Owa Bus Stop (大輪バス停). The trailhead begins just beside the bus stop; look for signs marked 三峰神社登山道 (Mitsumine Shrine Trail).

1 START AT OWA TRAILHEAD

Begin your ascent from Owa. The trail climbs gently through cedar and cypress, the forest floor damp with moss.

2 TENBO-DAI (VIEWPOINT REST)

After 2 hours of steady climbing, you'll reach a clearing with a panoramic view of the Chichibu Basin below.

3 MITSUMINE RIDGE WALK

The path undulates along the ridge, opening occasionally to glimpses of the Okuchichibu peaks.

4 ARRIVE AT MITSUMINE SHRINE

Mitsumine Shrine appears, framed by towering cryptomeria cedars. Its gate is guarded by okami (wolf statues), the shrine's divine protectors. Explore the ornate carvings, stone lanterns and serene inner courtyard.

5 LUNCH AT SHRINE AREA

There are small restaurants and rest houses near the shrine offering soba, oden and soft-serve ice cream flavoured with mountain herbs.

6 OPTIONAL RETURN

Descend the trail back to the Owa bus stop and catch the bus to Seibu-Chichibu Station. Alternatively, catch the bus from Owa bus stop to Mitsumineguchi Station, then take a local train back to Ohanabatake Station, which is a short walk from Seibu-Chichibu Station.

Advice → **Seasonal highlights:** spring for blossoms and autumn for foliage.

Check the bus timetable as the service can be infrequent: www.knet.ne.jp/~ats/eng/mb/m/mitu/miji.htm

Check mitsuminejinja.or.jp and www.chichibu-omotenashi.com for more advice and information.

There is another Mitsumine Shrine in the town centre, so please don't mix them up!

Chichibu Pilgrimage Day Walk

A day out visiting five of the 34 temples in the Chichibu area.

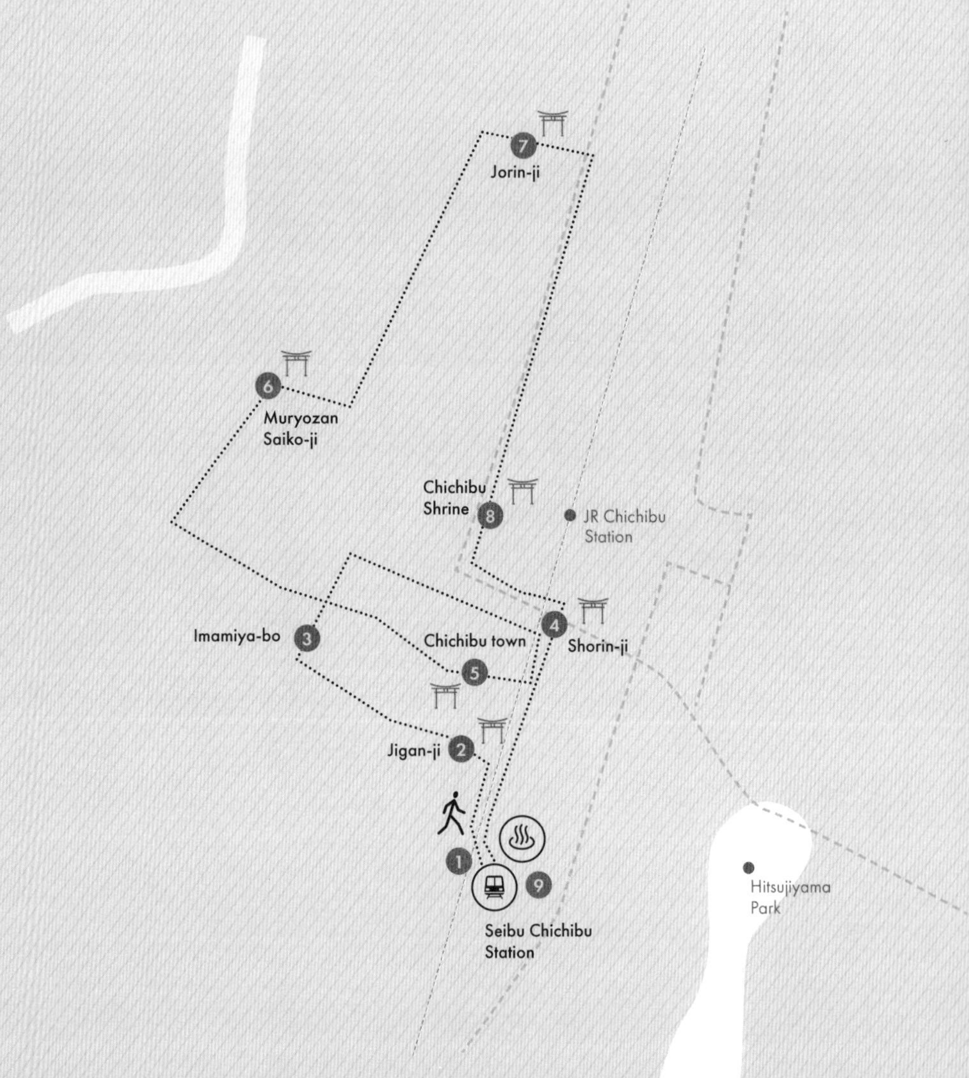

Distance: 8–10-kilometre (5–6-mile) loop | Difficulty: Easy to moderate

1 START AT SEIBU-CHICHIBU STATION

Exit the station and pick up a map from the tourist information centre. Many temples are clearly signposted with stone markers bearing the character 観音 (Kannon).

2 TEMPLE NO. 13: JIGAN-JI (慈眼寺)

Jigan-ji Temple is famous for its wooden hall with intricate carvings. People come here to pray for eye health.

3 TEMPLE NO. 14: IMAMIYA-BO (長岳山 今宮坊)

Imamiya-bo Temple is identified by its vermillion torii gate and a famous 'Flying Celestial Figure' statue, kneeling and holding a lotus stem.

4 TEMPLE NO. 15: SHORIN-JI (少林寺)

Next, make your way to **Shorin-ji**, a small temple also known for the intricate carvings in its main hall.

5 LUNCH IN TOWN

With three temples under your belt, walk back towards central Chichibu for lunch.

6 TEMPLE NO. 16: MURYOZAN SAIKO-JI (西光寺)

Built in 1710, the **Muryozan Saiko-ji Temple** contains replica images of the 88 Shikoku Pilgrimage temples.

7 TEMPLE NO. 17: JORIN-JI (定林寺)

Jorin-ji Temple is famous for its bell tower, cast in 1758.

8 CHICHIBU SHRINE (秩父神社)

End your walk at this vivid, centuries-old shrine in the heart of town.

9 RETURN TO SEIBU-CHICHIBU STATION

Relax with a soak at **Matsuri-no-Yu**, the hot spring beside the station, before taking the evening train back to Tokyo.

Advice → Seasonal highlights: spring for blossoms and autumn for foliage.

WEEKEND TRIPPER

Most of the listings in this book can be done as a day trip, but for places further afield we recommend packing your pyjamas and a toothbrush and turning your trip into a mini-break. The destinations in this chapter's sections are best enjoyed spread over a couple of days to make the most them. Evening streets quieten, lanterns glow, and the rhythm of a city shifts in ways that day trippers rarely witness. Staying overnight allows time for slow dinners, early morning walks and those serendipitous discoveries that happen when you are not watching the clock for the last train back to Tokyo.

The elegant castle town of Kanazawa rewards those who linger with its beautifully preserved districts, traditional crafts and gardens that reveal different moods across the day. Further north, Niigata offers coastal air, renowned sake breweries and a food culture shaped by some of Japan's finest rice. To the west, the great urban duo of Osaka and Kyoto invites a deeper immersion. Osaka's neon-lit food streets and exuberant nightlife come alive after dark, while Kyoto reveals its quieter magic in its early morning temples and twilight alleyways.

These destinations can be done as day trips, and we have, on occasion, zipped over to Kyoto or Kanazawa for the day and had many a wonderful experience. However, a night or two away transforms these cities from quick sightseeing stops into places that can be truly absorbed.

MARUFUKURO HOTEL, KYOTO

NIIGATA

Once a vital trading port and gateway to the north, Niigata today feels both grounded and open – a prefecture of soft light, vast skies and deep hospitality. Yasunari Kawabata's *Snow Country* was partly set in Yuzawa in Niigata Prefecture. The novel's evocative paragraphs described the region so poetically that the area was etched in our psyche as a must-visit destination. Niigata and surrounds felt like a place we already knew the feeling, smell and taste of.

BANDAIJIMA FISH MARKET, P 221

Niigata is a place defined by water – snowmelt rushing from alpine peaks, rivers running through lush plains, waves lapping endlessly against the shore. Here, rice is more than sustenance; it is embedded in the culture, the precious grain being the basis for the region's famed sake.

The rhythm of life moves between paddies and ports, shrines and shorelines, from the slopes of Yahiko to the sands of Sado Island. It's on these fertile fields and paddies, still water reflecting the surrounding region like a mirror, that you can watch the sunset paint the coast in copper or explore the art fields across the hills of Echigo-Tsumari. Niigata is a little off the radar, and yet travelling here you'll find warmth, craftsmanship and the endless conversation between land and sea.

Another very good reason to travel to Niigata is to enjoy the Joetsu Shinkansen 2017 East Japan Rail's ekiben winner, Ebi Senryo Chirashi, a bento box stuffed with eel, squid and lobster under a fluffy omelette.

Advice → *Don't miss Niigata's famous Jomon-style pottery, in particular the Flame Pottery. Ceramics and workshops are available at Aotogama Studio.*

SEAFOOD & SAKE IN NIIGATA CITY

A festive fish market and an historical sake brewery

~2 hr

20 min

20 min

GETTING THERE

From Tokyo Station, take the Joetsu Shinkansen to Niigata Station (~2 hours). Take the North exit to the Bandaijima Fresh Fish Market (20 min). Walk from the Fish Market to Imoyamatsukasa (20 min). Or walk from Niigata Station to Imoyamatsukasa (15 min).

imayotsukasa.co.jp

DISCOVER

Bandaijima Fresh Fish Market and food stalls; Imayo Tsukasa Sake Brewery – brewery tours with English guides (book ahead), a tasting room with premium junmai daiginjo and seasonal brews, traditional wooden fermentation vats and cold-cellar rooms; local Niigata rice sake and ceramics.

SEASONAL HIGHLIGHTS

Autumn: food and sake pairing, harvest festivals. Winter: sake-brewing season.

Advice → *Try pairing sake with local dishes such as hegi soba, snow crab or sasa dango.*

A trip to **Niigata** – a city shaped by salt air, snowmelt water and some of Japan's finest seafood and sake – delivers a clean, delicious break from Tokyo's pace . The Shinkansen covers the distance in just under 2 hours, trading towers for rice fields and revealing a landscape where snowy winters and coastal abundance define the flavour of the region.

Near the port, **Bandaijima Fresh Fish Market** is perfect in the early morning, setting a lively tone with its festival-like energy. Outside, charcoal grills flare and crackle; oysters open with a soft sigh as their shells heat; scallops caramelise over open flame; skewered river fish – often sweet, fragrant ayu – stand like little flags in the glowing coals. Inside the market, bright rows of sashimi glisten beside towers of crab and trays of uni. A grocery section stocks local pickles and dried seafood, and a liquor store highlights regional specialties. Come hungry – this is Niigata at its most immediate and edible.

Niigata's deeper character, however, is shaped by snow. The region's famed sake owes its clarity to cold winters, soft water from rivers, such as the Agano, and rice polished to a pearly sheen. At **Imayo Tsukasa Sake Brewery**, established in 1767, tradition resides in cedar-scented kura buildings where brewing follows a slow, deliberate rhythm. Guided tours (advance reservation recommended) trace the process from steaming rice to fermenting mash, revealing a craft refined over centuries. Tastings explore the region's spectrum of styles: crisp, mineral junmai; elegant daiginjo with delicate apple and pear notes; smooth brews shaped by the quiet alchemy of snowmelt and patience. Those without time for the full tour can opt for a focused tasting session – a concentrated 30-minute all-you-can-taste dive into Niigata sake's distinctive, clean profile, which includes Japan's prize-winning Koshihikari Junmai. Before leaving, sample the sake lees soft-serve ice cream: creamy, lightly sweet and unmistakably local.

Back at Niigata Station, **Ponshukan** offers one more immersion. A wall of more than 100 regional sake labels awaits, with token-operated tasting machines allowing small, curated sips. Each pour hints at a different landscape: a mountain snowfall, a cold river, the hush of winter fields.

A Niigata sleep over is a story written in salt and snow – fresh seafood pulled from the Sea of Japan, sake shaped by winter purity. Settle into cosy accomodation near the Shinano River or overlooking the ocean. By the time the train slides back towards Tokyo, your bags may be heavy with sake bottles (regional craft is also remarkable), but the real souvenir is the lingering memory of flavours drawn straight from Niigata's land and sea.

今代司
今代司の
日本酒定期便

別館 立食い 弁慶

ART & NATURE IN ECHIGO-TSUMARI ART FIELDS

Nature as a canvas

Shinkansen		90 min
Train		~35 min
Bike		hire a bike
OR Car		hire a car

GETTING THERE

From Tokyo Station, take the Joetsu Shinkansen to Echigo-Yuzawa Station (90 min). To explore nearby art by bicycle, take the Hokuhoku Line to Tokamachi Station or Matsudai Station (~35 min), then hire a bike from outside the stations. To visit far-flung art, hire a car from outside Echigo-Yuzawa Station.

echigo-tsumari.jp

DISCOVER

Tunnel of Light by Ma Yansong/ MAD Architects at Kiyotsu Gorge, *House of Light* by James Turrell, 'Matsudai Nobutai' art platform, rice terraces, seasonal Echigo-Tsumari Art Triennale (every three years).

SEASONAL HIGHLIGHTS

Summer to early autumn: art in the greenest fields. Winter: snow sculptures and installations.

Advice → *Rent a car or e-bike to explore remote installations spread across more than 200 villages. E-bikes can be rented at Tokamachi Station from late April to November.*

Between the mountains of **Tokamachi** and **Tsunan**, art is not something hung on walls; it forms, seemingly organically, from the land itself. The **Echigo-Tsumari Art Field**, launched in 2000, reimagines and reshapes rural life with more than 100 artworks distributed across rice terraces, villages and forests. A major drawcard of the area is the land itself, in particular the rice fields in the winter mist or at sunset, and the snow-powdered mountains. Here, art stands boldly in the open or remains secretive, ready to be discovered.

In the **Kiyotsu Gorge**, *Tunnel of Light* by Ma Yansong/ MAD Architects transforms stone into space-age reverie, a corridor that ends in an infinity mirror of sky and river. Further north, not far from Tokamachi, James Turrell's *House of Light* is a meditation on impermanence and change: shifting illuminations and water are set in a house, aglow at night. In Hachi Village, **Hachi & Seizo Tashima Museum of Picture Book Art** transforms a former elementary school into a cosy picture-book story.

Art lovers gather at the fields during the famous **Echigo-Tsumari Art Triennale**. Every piece here feels like an act of remembering – the farmers, the floods, the snows, the days. You leave not only inspired, but humbled by the gentle persistence of the land and the responsive and reflective nature of art. During the trienniale, art is placed across an area covering 760 square kilometres (293 square miles).

Tokamachi is an accessible location from which to explore many of the art pieces. You can hire a bike from outside Tokamachi Station or Matsudai Station or walk to several artworks nearby. Staying overnight will enable you to fit in more art that might further afield. If going as a day trip, stick to **Matsudai** and explore what art you can; there are quite a few easily accessible pieces (note that **Matsudai Castle** is now an excellent contemporary art gallery). *House of Light* is about 2 kilometres (1 mile) from Gejo Station, two stops north of Tokamachi Station, and *Tunnel of Light* is about 20 kilometres (12 miles) south of Tokamachi Station.

Some artworks also double as unique overnight accomodation. *Shedding House*, *Dream House*, *Australia House* and *House of Light* all offer different experiences at varying price points.

HIKING MOUNT HAGURO

A pilgrimage of rebirth and a spectacular pagoda

3 hr

40 min

GETTING THERE

From Niigata Station, take the Inaho Limited Express train to Tsuruoka Station (3 hr). From the station's north exit, take the bus to Dewa Sanzan Shrine (40 min).

dewasanzan.jp

DISCOVER

Over 2400 stone steps through cedar forest to Mount Haguro's summit, the five-storey pagoda of Haguro (a national treasure), Shukubo Temple lodgings for pilgrims.

SEASONAL HIGHLIGHTS

Spring: abundant greenery.
Autumn: fiery leaves.

Advice → *Wear sturdy shoes and bring a small bell – the sound keeps both bears and bad spirits away.*

Mist coils around the cedars of **Mount Haguro**, oldest of the **Three Sacred Mountains of Dewa**, where pilgrims have sought rebirth for centuries. Each stone step has felt the footfall of many a traveller, the air is a symphony of running water and birdsong, and each breath fills with incense.

Early on in your trek, the forest opens up and small shrines line the path. A wooden bridge spans a small river fed by a picturesque waterfall. Not far from here, the **five-storey pagoda of Haguro** rises like a dream from the forest floor, a sublime tower of rain-darkened wood, ornate carvings and silent majesty.

The ascent itself is part of the experience. The moss-softened stairway — some 2400 stone steps laid in the 17th century — winds beneath towering cryptomeria trees, several said to be over a thousand years old. Along the route stand dozens of small shrines and stone markers, reminders that this mountain has long been a place of devotion rather than spectacle. In winter, the forest lies deep under snow; in summer, cool mist drifts through the cedars, making the climb feel like you're entering a living temple. If you have time, linger in the quiet of the mountain after the day visitors have left – it is one of the most memorable experiences in the region.

This is where monks once underwent Shugendo training – an ascetic practice blending Buddhism, Shinto and mountain worship. Today, travellers still climb for silence and reflection. At the top of Mount Haguro, before you begin your descent, whether by bus or on foot, stroll the grounds of the expansive, tranquil **Sanjin Gosaiden Shrine**.

We recommend staying at a Shukubo pilgrimage inn for an atmospheric and restful night.

KANAZAWA

Day trip, overnighter or weekender – the Hokuriku Shinkansen brings this gold-leafed city closer than you might realise. Kanazawa is a place where beauty resides in the details – a golden thread weaving together history, art and the sea. Once the domain of the powerful Maeda clan, it grew not through conquest but through culture, nurturing artisans, poets and tea masters. Today, its spirit endures in the shimmer of gold leaf, the stillness of Kenroku-en Garden and the craftsmanship of its markets and ateliers. Walk its streets and you'll find a living museum – Edo-era samurai lanes beside sleek modern museums, lacquerware beside latte art, silence beside snow. Kanazawa's rhythm is unhurried; its elegance, understated. Whether you come for the seafood at Omicho Market, to try your hand at a centuries-old craft, or simply to watch the rain cloak the city in silver light, Kanazawa invites you to slow down and see – truly see – how art, tea, the sea and the land intertwine.

KENROKU-EN GARDEN, P 237

We often like to spend Christmas in Japan. Much debate goes on as to what our perfect Christmas lunch will be. One year, with a day left on our Japan Rail passes, a unanimous decision was made to have a sushi Christmas lunch at Omicho Market in Kanazawa. We caught the Hokuriku Shinkansen north, watching snow fall over the plains. Arriving in Kanazawa, we lunched on a tuna bowl flecked with gold leaf, followed by a 'Japanese Christmas pudding' (wagashi from nearby store Ohako) and some huge Noto Peninsula strawberries. Our Christmas toast was with Ishikawa sake, cold and clean, born of the snow's meltwater. We followed this with a stroll through Kenroku-en Garden, then headed back to Tokyo. Without doubt, it was one of the best Christmases ever.

SEAFOOD, SOY & SALT IN KANAZAWA

The sea's bounty in a golden city

2.5 hr

6 min

OR

15 min

GETTING THERE

From Tokyo Station, take the Hokuriku Shinkansen to Kanazawa Station (2.5 hr). For Omicho Market, from the station's Kenroku-en exit, take the Kanazawa Loop bus to Musashigatsuji Bus Stop (6 min) or walk from the station to the market (15 min).

visitkanazawa.jp

DISCOVER

Omicho Market, Ishikawa Local Products Center, Yamato Soy Sauce & Miso Company, Noto salt from Shinkai Salt, Ishikawa sake breweries.

SEASONAL HIGHLIGHTS

Spring: Noto strawberries.
Autumn: matsutake mushrooms.
Winter: snow crab and buri (yellowtail).

Advice → *Anto at Kanazawa Station is a treasure trove of regional specialties and edible delights, so leave time to explore before you board the train.*

Kanazawa is a city that tastes of tides and snowmelt – a place where the Sea of Japan and the mountains collaborate in every bowl, every sip, every scent drifting from a market stall. For a food-driven weekend away from Tokyo, few places reward appetite and curiosity quite like this golden city.

Begin where Kanazawa has fed itself for centuries: **Omicho Market**. Established in the Edo period, it still beats to the rhythm of the sea. The air hums with hawkers' banter, knives tapping, the ocean laid out in every imaginable form – snow crab, gleaming nodoguro, translucent sweet shrimp, thick ribbons of yellowtail, oysters so cold they taste like winter. Some fish look positively prehistoric – an education for foodies and citizen scientists alike.

Stallholders tuck small counters into the lanes, offering seafood as raw as morning light or charred over crackling grills. Bowls of kaisen-don arrive as edible mosaics: ruby tuna, buttery scallops, sweet ebi – often crowned with Kanazawa's signature flourish, a glimmer of gold leaf. Sushi in the market is unforgettable, the kind that rewrites your experience of freshness.

A 20-minute walk away from the market, the **Ishikawa Local Products Center** brings together the flavours that shape this region. Shelves glow with soy sauce and miso from **Yamato Soy Sauce & Miso Company**, first established in 1911, their brews aged slow and deep in cedar vats. Look for Noto salt from **Shinkai Salt**, harvested by hand on the rugged peninsula (now part of ongoing efforts to support coastal communities rebuilding after the 2024 earthquake).

For sweetness, Kanazawa delivers with equal poetry: Noto strawberries, vivid and fragrant; and the exquisite wagashi of **Morihachi**, confectioners since 1625, who capture the seasons in bean paste and sugar.

Food leads naturally to drink here. Ishikawa Prefecture is a sake powerhouse, and lunch invites a slow glass – perhaps Tengumai, earthy and expressive, or Kagatobi, clean and mineral like the meltwater that feeds the region's breweries. Each sip folds mountains, water and time together.

Staying overnight allows you to spend time with all of Kanazawa's pleasures and revisit the market to try seafood you were too full to fit in the first time around. Before catching the Shinkansen home, wander the **Kanazawa Station food hall**, a wonderland of regional goods and some of Japan's finest ekiben– boxed meals filled to the brim with local crab, pickles and superb-quality rice – perfect companions for the homeward ride. When your train hums back to Tokyo, your bags will be full of soy, salt and the lingering faint perfume of strawberries.

KANAZAWA'S ARTISAN HERITAGE

A touch of gold

2.5 hr

17 min

GETTING THERE

From Tokyo Station, take the Hokuriku Shinkansen to Kanazawa Station (2.5 hr). From Kanazawa Station's Kenroku-en exit, take the Kanazawa Loop bus (Right Loop) to the 21st Century Museum Stop (17 min).

kanazawa-museum.jp

DISCOVER

Kanazawa Yasue Gold Leaf Museum, gold leaf workshops, Kanazawa lacquerware studios, mizuhiki craft, Yanagi Sori Memorial Museum.

SEASONAL HIGHLIGHTS

All seasons; rainy days are perfect for gold and lacquer workshops.

Advice → *Book experiences in advance – small workshops fill fast.*

Anto shopping area at Kanazawa Station sells kutani-yaki (regional ceramics) and Kanazawa-shikki (regional laquerware).

Kanazawa has long been a city where beauty grows quietly – not in monuments of power, but in the patient rhythm of hands at work. The Maeda clan, who governed the region during the Edo period, poured their wealth into culture rather than battle, nurturing artisans whose descendants still shape the city's identity. While other domains refined their swords, Kanazawa refined its crafts: gleaming lacquer, gold leaf pressed thin as air, paper twisted into symbolic knots strong enough to hold prayers.

A craft-focused day unfolds like slipping into a living atelier. The **Kanazawa Yasue Gold Leaf Museum** offers the perfect beginning – a place where metal becomes light. Exhibits chart the improbable transformation of gold beaten to one-ten-thousandth of a millimetre – leaves so delicate they flutter with the faintest breath. Tools, screens and century-old techniques reveal why Kanazawa produces over 99 per cent of Japan's gold leaf. Each display feels like watching sunlight learn to take shape.

In the deep calm of **Kanazawa lacquerware (shikki) studios**, the craft moves at an entirely different tempo. Layer upon layer of urushi sap is brushed, cured and polished; hours, days and weeks collapse into a single perfect sheen. Some studios offer short maki-e experiences, allowing visitors to sprinkle gold or silver powder over fresh lacquer.

Just across town, another art reveals Kanazawa's quieter heart. Mizuhiki craft – ceremonial cords made from tightly twisted washi paper – turns simplicity into elegance. Workshops at stores such as **Hiraoka Yuinou-ho** or **Mizuhiki Accessory Workshop Kanazawa Kurumi** teach you how to loop and fold the cords into knots symbolising fortune, connection and gratitude. The results are small but meaningful: a charm for a suitcase or a tie for a gift, letter or hair ornament, a reminder that beauty often resides in restraint.

Stepping deeper into Kanazawa's design lineage, the **Yanagi Sori Memorial Museum** celebrates one of Japan's most influential industrial designers. Yanagi Sori's father, Yanagi Soetsu, was instrumental in the establishment of the folk crafts movement in Japan. Yanagi's philosophy – utility enriched by grace – echoes everywhere in Kanazawa's craft culture.

A day here becomes a pilgrimage to the handmade: gold, lacquer, paper, memory. The city does not simply display its craft; it invites you into the rhythm of its making, letting the past form gently in your hands like leaf-light, lacquer-shine and cinched knot.

A TRANQUIL DAY IN KANAZAWA

Paths of reflection

2.5 hr

10 min

GETTING THERE

From Tokyo Station, take the Hokuriku Shinkansen to Kanazawa Station (2.5 hr). From Kanazawa Station's Kenroku-en exit, take the Kanazawa Loop bus to Kenroku-en Garden (10 min). Begin the hike at the garden's Katsurazaka Gate.

DISCOVER

Kenroku-en Garden, Ishikawa Gate, Asano River, Miharashidai Observation Deck, Utatsuyama Park, D.T. Suzuki Museum.

SEASONAL HIGHLIGHTS

Spring: sakura. Autumn: the flame of maples.

Advice → *The full loop – Kenroku-en Garden to Mount Utatsu – takes 50–60 minutes; bring comfortable walking shoes and water.*

Kenroku-en Garden is more than one of Japan's Three Great Gardens; it is a poem that unfurls across hills, ponds, lanterns and ancient pines. Kenroku-en translates as 'Garden of Six Attributes'. Created and perfected over centuries by the Maeda clan, this vast strolling garden embodies six classical virtues (attributes) of Japanese landscape design: spaciousness, seclusion, artifice, antiquity, water views and sweeping panoramas. Together, they form a world so harmonious it almost feels imaginary, like you have wandered into a dream where nature itself paused to admire its reflection in **Kasumigaike Pond**.

Paths curl gently through miniature forests, across stone bridges, past teahouses. It is a garden calibrated to light – morning gold through cedar branches, afternoon shadows sliding across moss, the low amber illumination that settles over the landscape in the darker hours. Each season transforms Kenroku-en Garden utterly. Spring brings a cascading blush of cherry blossoms, petals drifting across ponds, soft confetti. In early summer, irises flare purple at the water's edge. Autumn is our favourite time: crimson maples, burnished ginkgo and leaves that roll out red carpets across the grass, draping the garden in theatrical splendour. Winter is pure enchantment – fresh snow muffles sound, lanterns glow softly and the iconic yukizuri ropes fan out from the pines like delicate webs, protecting the ancient branches under their snowy burden.

The teahouses alone could occupy an afternoon's wandering. **Miyoshian**, tucked near the river, feels like a retreat from the world, a place to sip matcha while watching reflections ripple across the water. **Suitei**, with its graceful silhouette and views over carefully framed scenery, is a study in serene fairytale-like beauty. **Uchihashi-tei**, poised elegantly above the pond on stilts, is the garden's heart – a teahouse that seems to float, offering a vantage point into Kenrokuen Garden's most painterly compositions.

Everywhere, details whisper of centuries of care: stone lanterns softened by lichen, winding streams fed by ingenious Edo-period waterworks, islands shaped like tortoises and cranes for longevity, sculpted pines trained by generations of gardeners and volunteers (friends of the garden). Even the breeze carries history, drifting through trees that have stood sentinel for hundreds of years.

A ZEN NATURE WALK

From the garden's **Katsurazaka Gate**, cross through the **Ishikawa Gate**, past the impressive dark gables and looming white walls of **Kanazawa Castle** and out, heading north to the **Chaya district** and the **Asano River**, its surface reflecting wooden bridges and open sky. Follow the narrow lanes, climbing uphill past increasingly impressive town views, until you reach **Utatsuyama Park**, where the air grows stiller, the sound of the city replaced by the soft rustle of bamboo and grass. Take time to explore the park. The **Hanashobu-en** is a mini-wetland soundtracked with chirping birds and croaking frogs. A rustic gravel and stone staircase goes through a torii gate to **Atago Shrine**. Memorable views can be found at **Overlook Hill**. From there climb to **Miharashidai Observation Deck** and gaze out – Kanazawa spreads below like a painted fan, with tiled roofs, temple spires, the distant shimmer of the Sea of Japan.

Descend from the park towards the **Tokiwa Bridge** and cross it before making your way southwest to the **D.T. Suzuki Museum**, which welcomes you with glass, light and silence. Here the great Buddhist philosopher is celebrated with works, artefacts and exhibits. This is where philosophy and landscape meet, the beauty of impermanence, the shimmer of what remains. The stand-out moment comes when you walk out to the **Contemplation Space**. Taniguchi Yoshio's architectural marvel is an open-sided meditation cube suspended in still water that ripples at timed intervals, symbolising the creation of ideas. Walkways let you stroll to the centre and meditate in the **Water Mirror Garden**, the glistening metallic cube beaming in serene energy from the cosmos. As an extra treat, head to **Shofukaku Garden**. By **Kasumigaike Pond** you'll find a small door that leads to a platform, where you can look out onto the Water Mirror Garden and Contemplation Space from a different angle.

KANSAI

The region of Kansai is considered by many to be the jewel of Japan. Cities such as Kyoto and Nara were spared from World War II bombings and have a plethora of memorable temples, gardens and places of astounding age and beauty. Much of Osaka was destroyed in the war, and as a result it is largely a contemporary city, though you can still find pockets of old Japan, especially from the samurai era of the Edo period (1603–1868).

HONEN-IN TEMPLE, P 244

Both Kyoto and Nara were once the capital cities of Japan, and are places of great cultural importance. Kyoto alone has more than 1600 temples and shrines. Osaka, in contrast, is a frenetic, contemporary city with many of its own particular quirks and points of interest. As Japan's popularity grows, these cities in Kansai are high on most travellers' to-do lists. Our hope here is to show you a different side of Kansai – one where you can wander at your own pace, absorbing the atmosphere on the streets, while having a varied itinerary that takes you to less-visited places that we know and love.

INCENSE IN KYOTO

A weekend of history, scent and reflection

2 hr 40 min

GETTING THERE

From Tokyo Station, take the Tokaido Shinkansen to Kyoto Station (2 hr 40 min). Take exit 2.

DISCOVER

Rokkaku-do Temple; Shoyeido Kyoto Main Store; Kyukyodo Honte; Owariya Incense; Sanjusangen-do, Honen-in, Ginkaku-ji and Nanzen-ji temples.

SEASONAL HIGHLIGHTS

All seasons are good for visiting Kyoto.

Advice → *If you have a JR pass, you cannot travel on the super-fast Nozomi Shinkansen to Kyoto and Shin-Osaka without paying a supplement fee. Alternatively, the Hikari Shinkansen departs Tokyo Station every 30 minutes and takes 2 hours 40 minutes, as opposed to the Nozomi train, which takes 2 hours 20 minutes.*

Japan's love of incense began in the 6th century CE. However, it wasn't until the Heian Period (794–1185 CE) that Murasaki Shikibu, in her novel *The Tale of Genji* (considered to be the first novel in the world and set in the imperial court in Kyoto), depicted incense as a practice. Deeply tied to Zen Buddhism, incense releases smoky aromas that waft around creating a heady scent, an evocation of nature. It is used in religious ceremonies to purify spaces. In the Muromachi period (1336–1573) it was one of the classical arts known as the Way of Incense, which ranks alongside crafts such as ikebana and tea ceremony.

Incense is deeply tied to reflection and meditation; these are the key reasons why we burn incense in our home every day, choosing scents based on mood, the weather or the tasks we are performing. Burning incense is also one of our favourite ways to remember a holiday, and nothing evokes memories more than the complex beauty of a scent floating through our house that recalls the temple or garden where it was bought. When in Tokyo, if we have a day left on our rail pass, we will plan a day trip to Kyoto so we can have a mindful day wandering streets and temples, stopping at favourite spots to replenish our incense supply. Here's one of our favourite itineraries, based on our love of incense.

A SENSORY ITINERARY

From Kyoto Station, catch the Karasuma Line train to Karasuma Station to find contemporary incense brand **Lisn**. Interior designers and fans of colour-blocking will especially love this futuristic store of architectural waveforms. If you find it hard to choose a favourite scent from their extensive range, their trial sets provide you with a selection. We love the Green range (which includes Norwegian Wood and Monster Tree), Michi from the Oriental range and Natty from the Classical range.

Next, walk up Karasuma-dori and turn onto Rokkaku-dori to **Rokkaku-do Temple**, the home of Steve's favourite incense. When we burn it at home, the aroma always reminds us of this little temple (where, incidentally, Ikenobo Ikebana was founded in Japan). Make your way back to Karasuma-dori and the incredibly beautiful old incense store **Shoyeido Kyoto Main Store**, a brand that dates to 1705. Suppliers to Buddhist temples, their classical and unique fragrance combinations are deeply rooted in history. The Horin Discovery Set includes our favourite scent: City of Culture (Muromachi).

Next, float up and along Ebisugawa-dori, then down Teramachi-dori to incense and stationery store **Kyukyodo Honten**. Dating to 1594, the store's own fragrance, Teramachi 705, is a lovely keepsake. Or try another one of our favourites, Matsuo no Koke, or the Sakura scent. Next head to Keihan Sanjo Station to visit nearby **Owariya Incense**. Their round incense balls, made to scent drawers and cupboards, are a unique take on fragrance and make a wonderful gift.

Back at Keihan Sanjo Station, catch the train to Keihan Shichijo Station, where you'll find **Sanjusangen-do Temple** with its woody, smoky incense that is another of Steve's favourites (and, yes, the temple is pretty spectacular too!). If you have an extra day, or started early, there are three other places (also exceptional temples) for fine incense: **Honen-in Temple**, which is the resting place of one of our most cherished Japanese authors, Jun'ichiro Tanizaki, who wrote *In Praise of Shadows*; **Ginkaku-ji Temple**; and **Nanzen-ji Temple**.

UNCOVER NARA'S DEEP HISTORY

Culture and contemplation in Japan's first capital

2 hr 40 min

45–60 min

GETTING THERE

From Tokyo Station, take the Tokaido Shinkansen to Kyoto Station (2 hr 40 min), then take the JR Nara Line or Kintetsu Line to Nara Station (45–60 min). Take the east exit.

DISCOVER

Naramachi Koshi-no-Ie, National Historic Site of Zuto, Nara Kasugano International Forum Iraka, Daijo-in Temple Garden Cultural Hall, roaming deer, Camphor Tree on Sagihara Road, Goryo Shrine, Kasuga Taisha, Meoto Daikokusha, Todai-ji Temple.

SEASONAL HIGHLIGHTS

All seasons are good for visiting Nara.

Advice → *Nara is known for its craft, including excellent yarn, and for its mochi – watch experts pounding the dough in stores along the main street.*

While a day trip to **Nara** is possible from Tokyo, consider turning it into a Kansai mini-break for a more relaxed jaunt. This region has an incredible amount of culture and beauty. Nara was Japan's first capital, giving its name to the Nara period, an 84-year era during which, among other great achievements, literature and poetry flourished. Modern-day Nara is in itself a history lesson, with **Todai-ji Temple** one of Japan's most revered and significant places to visit. Our itinerary below shows a quieter side of this great city, now popular with visitors. It's a walk and a history lesson through Nara, a multi-stop itinerary that you can adapt or dip in and out of as you'd like.

A WANDERING ITINERARY

Begin the day in Nara with something warm and grounding. **Fujimon Seimen**, set inside a beautifully preserved historic building, serves morning ramen with a choice of pork or fish that feels both fortifying and deeply local – springy noodles, rising steam and the sense that you're stepping into a story that began long before you arrived.

If you're an earlier riser, it's worth beginning instead in **Naramachi**, where the gentle wooden structure of **Goryo Shrine** waits in the morning hush. Open 24 hours, it's small, local and utterly unhurried. It invites a kind of soft attention – a moment to breathe before the day unfurls.

A short walk away, **Naramachi Koshi-no-Ie (Lattice House)** offers a window into Edo-period daily life. This faithful reconstruction reveals how merchants once lived in these narrow machiya homes, all latticed facades, slender corridors and inner gardens that catch the sun.

From here, wander towards the **Daijo-in Temple Garden Cultural Hall**, where a serene pond, an arched bridge and carefully tended plantings create a miniature world for nature lovers. The stillness stays with you as you continue on to the **National Historic Site of Zuto**, a Buddhist monument built in 767 CE. With its tiered, pyramidal form and faintly worn stone buddhas, it belies the usual dome shape of Buddhist stupas and feels like a secret whispered across time.

Keep walking along quiet paths until you reach the ancient and astonishing **Camphor Tree on Sagihara Road**. Said to be more than 1500 years old, standing before it, you feel as if the tree itself remembers every footstep ever taken beneath its boughs.

When it's time to pause, the **Nara Kasugano International Forum Iraka** offers a stylish oasis of architecture and gardens. Deer roam the grounds with practised grace, and the garden – often missed by visitors – reveals itself slowly.

Your next stop is one of the loveliest secrets in all of Japan: **Mizuya Chaya**, a thatched-roof fairytale hut nestled in the forest clearing. Udon, tea and traditional sweets taste different here – softer somehow, enriched by surrounding moss, cedar and birdsong.

Refreshed, wander towards the vermillion corridors of **Kasuga Taisha**, where thousands of lanterns line your path and monks drift past in quiet concentration. Couples should stop at **Meoto Daikokusha**, a sub-shrine dedicated to love, partnership and the hope of a harmonious life.

Keep going beneath the shifting canopy and you'll eventually arrive at the edge of the **Kasugayama Primeval Forest**, a sacred and ancient woodland. Step inside and the world seems to melt away – paths winding into green shadow, spirits breathing in the leaves. Walk too far and you may never wish to return ...

EAT YOUR WAY AROUND OSAKA

Street food with soul

2 hr 55 min

20 min

GETTING THERE

From Tokyo Station, take the Tokaido Shinkansen to Shin-Osaka Station (2 hr 55 min), then take the Midosuji Metro Line to Namba Station (20 min). Take exit 14.

kuromon.com/en

DISCOVER

Kuromon Ichiba Market, Shinsekai, Dotonbori and Namba.

SEASONAL HIGHLIGHTS

All seasons are good for visiting Osaka.

Advice → *You can easily flit between Kyoto, Nara and Osaka as they are all in close proximity.*

Osaka lives life large. It's bright, bubbly, fun and just a little bit messy. No wonder it's Japan's self-proclaimed street food capital! Sure, there is a wonderful castle, one of the world's best aquariums and Harry Potter World, but if you're visiting for just one day or overnight, why not go on a culinary tour of the city's fresh, delicious and affordable array of street food. Yes, we always suggest you get an ekiben for the train, but this time save your appetite for a serious day of grazing and walking.

Many street food stalls have over-the-top signage (think oversize octopus peering down at you or giant dragon wrapping its way around a building), so it can be an assault on all your senses. Osaka-centric street and fast foods include kushikatsu (fried food on sticks, including meat, seafood and vegetables, such as lotus root, dipped into sauces), takoyaki (octopus-stuffed balls of dough, fried in a special pan and covered with mayonnaise) and okonomiyaki (Osaka's version of a pancake filled with cabbage and an assortment of vegetables, seafood and meat). Many of these street food experiences can be found in the **Dotonbori** district and around **Namba**, so spend some time wandering and snacking here, but there are many other places to explore. It's a good idea to bring yen with you as many market stalls and small eateries only take cash.

A STREET FOOD ITINERARY

As soon as you hop off the train at Shin-Osaka Station, jump on the Midosuji Metro Line to Namba Station, then take Exit 4 to **Kuromon Ichiba Market**, a dream destination for foodies. Enjoy fresh seafood delicacies such as uni (sea urchin), oysters, tiny octopus on sticks, giant crab legs and scallops grilled in their shells. Duck inside one of the many small eateries for a plate of fresh sushi or sashimi. Meat lovers should not miss the Kobe beef skewers. While the price may be higher than other market snacks, this meat is known for its superior quality.

The market is a one-stop foodie shop for all your Osaka favourites and includes tiny stalls selling takoyaki and kushikatsu. Michelle's picks for vegetarians are the superb range of pickles on offer, fresh tofu and soy milk from **Takahashi Shokuhin**, seasonal fruit and **Mitoya's** delicious mochi stuffed with fresh strawberries. Finish your feast with a soft-serve ice cream available in all of the flavours, including black sesame, matcha, dairy-free soy, mochi and yuzu, and pair it with a cold matcha from **Shiki Japanese Tea**.

If you made an early start at the market and would like to keep the snacking going, jump back on the Midosuji Line to Dobutsuen-mae Station and take Exit 1 or 5 for **Shinsekai**. The extremely photogenic streets and the quaintly vintage **Tsutenkaku Tower** make this area a visual delight, but it is also a place to discover street food vendors and small eateries. Our favourite place for takoyaki is **Fumichan**, though you'll want to swing by **Aji no Diamaru** for their festive atmosphere and larger-than-life octopus sign.

We think Shinsekai is the very best place to try kushikatsu, and there are many rough-and-tumble eateries that serve fried food on sticks with a beer or two. Our favourites are **Kushikatsu Daruma** with its iconic sign and delicious snack offerings (try their giant shrimp or quail eggs), with **Kushikatsu Shinsekai** and **Kikuyu** offering up some of the tastiest bites in the city. Expect the occasional strange choice, like fried grasshoppers, cicadas or camembert. Why not give one of them a try?

VINTAGE, FLEA & CRAFT MARKETS

Kyoto

- Kitano Tenmangu Shrine flea market (25th of each month)
- Kamigamo Shrine Craft Market (fourth Sunday of each month)
- To-ji Temple flea market (21st of each month)

Nara

- Tenjin-san Shrine Market (25th of each month)

Osaka

- Shitenno-ji Antique Market (21st–22nd of each month)
- Kansai Nominoichi flea market at Expo '70 Commemorative Park (first weekend of December)
- Gokoku Market (dates vary, check online)

ABOUT THE AUTHORS

Steve Wide and Michelle Mackintosh have been happily obsessed with Japan since their first trip, in the late 1990s.

What began as a holiday quickly turned into a lifelong fascination. These days they refer to Japan as their 'home away from home', returning for long stretches each year in search of great food, unique museums, quiet temples, inspiring architecture and the perfect neighbourhood coffee.

Steve is a writer and DJ who hosts a long-running indie radio show in Naarm/ Melbourne. Over the years he has DJ'd, interviewed and toured with international bands, including Oasis, Wet Leg, Primal Scream, Johnny Marr and Fontaines D.C.

He has hosted nightclubs, written ten pop-culture books on music icons and produced six delightfully odd books for children.

Michelle is an award-winning book designer and illustrator who has written four books exploring analogue correspondence, thoughtful gifting and the gentle art of everyday Japanese inspiration. More recently, she has collaborated with textile artist Cat Rabbit to create *Fuzzy Feelings*, a children's picture book about how to navigate different emotions. Michelle regularly speaks about the role of design in Japanese culture and the craft of bookmaking. Her work has been exhibited in Tokyo.

Together, Steve and Michelle have written, designed, photographed and illustrated twelve books about Japan, including *Tokyo Precincts, Kyoto Pocket Precincts, Onsen of Japan, Mindfulness Travel Japan, Hidden Pockets in Kyoto, Train Japan* and *Tokyo Story*. Their books have been translated into multiple languages and continue to encourage readers to wander a little deeper.

Steve and Michelle live in Naarm/ Melbourne with their British shorthair cat, Enid, who has never been to Japan but has stayed in a few cat hotels, where she dreams of the bonito treats she will enjoy upon her return home.

ARIGATO

So many publishing experts are required to make a book. We are so blessed to work alongside the below people who we consider to be our publishing family and not just the team we work with.

To the sublime team at Smith Street Books, thank you for your unbelievable expertise. A huge thank you to supremo Paul McNally for your always-inspiring vision. To dear Lucy Heaver, our brilliant commissioning and project editor, thank you for believing in us and for your incredible creativity, thoughtfulness and generosity. You truely made DTT a pleasure to work on. To Alexandra Payne, whose guidance kept us on track (even when we wanted to take one more detour), thank you for your clever decision-making and overarching editorial prowess. Thanks also to the amazing Aisling Coughlan, Lucy Grant and Megan Cuthbert; and to Penny Mansley for exemplary proofreading.

To Megan Ellis, thank you for your unmatched typesetting and image work. We feel a sense of calm every time we know we are working with you. To Hiki Komura, thank you for your delicate touch in bringing the Japanese language to our books in a way that thoughtfully considers Western readers.

-

Thank you to the following people for their kind and generous support: Yuko Fujii from Visit Gunma; Miu Saito from Kikkoman; Craig Roberts from Visit Chiba; evam eva yamanashi; Sawanoi Ozawa Brewery; Ririko Inami from the Pola Museum of Art; and Maeda from Enoura Observatory.

-

To our lovely community of Japanophiles, thank you for all of your support; it means the world to us.

-

To the Mackintosh family, thank you to mum; Carolyn and family; and Andrew and family. To the Wide family, thank you to mum and Barry; Chris and family; Heather and family; and Tracy and family. Also thanks to the Yeung family: Olivia, Joel and May. To our dear friends Hiki and Ryo, thank you for always making our Japan trips extra special. To our fellow travel mates Mel and El; Tiffany, Kylie and Jane; and our other incredibly dear friends – thank you for accepting that a 'quick research trip' is code for getting lost on purpose and sending too many photos of food, forests and floating around.

In memory of Lawrence and Danny.

Smith Street Books

Published in 2026 by
Smith Street Books
Naarm (Melbourne) | Australia
smithstreetbooks.com

Distributed outside of ANZ,
North & Latin America
by Thames & Hudson Ltd.,
6–24 Britannia Street, London,
WC1X 9JD
thamesandhudson.com

EU Authorised Representative:
Interart S.A.R.L.
19 rue Charles Auray, 93500
Pantin, Paris, France
productsafety@thameshudson.co.uk; www.interart.fr

ISBN: 978-1-9235-0335-9

Smith Street Books respectfully acknowledges the Wurundjeri People of the Kulin Nation, who are the Traditional Owners of the land on which we work, and we pay our respects to their Elders past and present.

Publisher: Lucy Heaver
Editor: Alexendra Payne
Designer & illustrator: Michelle Mackintosh
Typesetter: Megan Ellis
Photographers: Steve Wide & Michelle Mackintosh
Proofreader: Penny Mansley
Production manager: Aisling Coughlan

Printed & bound in China by C&C Offset Printing Co., Ltd.

Book 484

10 9 8 7 6 5 4 3 2 1

MIX
Paper | Supporting responsible forestry
FSC www.fsc.org
FSC® C008047